As I read through the ma... nagging question, "Why did I not know this before?" kick into both the heart and the head as he presents a mixture of basic and profound material every Believer needs to know and implement in their life. Had I read this book at the beginning of my walk with God, I would have avoided pitfalls and bounded ahead rather than meandering along as I did. Thanks, Rick. Once again I have learned and grown from what you have shared.

— Dr. Tom Blackaby,
Lead Pastor, Author, Speaker

At Work Within is a thoughtfully written volume that contains the content, depth, and weight of writers in the tradition of Peterson and Guinness, yet with a readability that makes it accessible to a broader audience. Rick Osborne draws from his years of writing experience to clearly and succinctly convey the essential truth of God's eternal desire to mold us into the image of His Son, Jesus Christ. Rick places the emphasis for this process clearly on the one who starts it and finishes it, God Himself. This is not another book about discipleship or growing in Christ that will leave you feeling guilty and unworthy. This is an account of the Good News of God at work in our lives. Rick compassionately illustrates the biblical narrative of hope and encouragement from the perspective of a fellow sojourner. This book will leave you in greater awe of God's grace and greater appreciation for His sovereignty and His work in your life.

— Todd Martin, Ph.D.
Sociologist, Author, Speaker, and former Pastor

I found this book immensely helpful, because it has a powerful grace-filled message from beginning to end. It relentlessly urges you to trust yourself completely to God's love and to believe that your heavenly Father longs to transform you from the inside-out—all His doing, by pure, undeserved mercy. I had a powerful epiphany while meditating on what Rick said, and therefore eagerly look forward to his next book.

— Ed Strauss,
Author/co-author of 54 devotional and apologetics books

"Go and make disciples." It seems simple, but are we doing what Jesus intended? Rick masterfully reminds us of the call, shows us biblically what was meant, and encourages us to action. Let Rick remind you of how Jesus disciples and helps us make disciples, by His Spirit, power, and grace "at work within" us.

— Rob Scott
Lead PastorKinnaired Park Community Church

If you want a strong bridge to where God wants you to be, read this book!

— Rhonda VanZuylekom

We may be the most informed yet least transformed generation of Christians history has seen, struggling to love and serve Jesus Christ while disconnected from full communion with Him. We know about him, but scarcely know Him. At Work Within connects our branches securely to the Vine so the transformative power of Jesus Christ can flow dynamically into our lives. This book is a must-read for every believer who wants to know and experience the Son of God intimately and consistently for themselves.

— Michael Q. Pink
Author

At Work Within

At Work Within

Be transformed into all God created you to be

For God is working in you, giving you the desire to obey him, and the power to do what pleases him.
Philippians 2:13 NLT

Rick Osborne

impartation idea inc.
Publishing Heaven's Heart

Published by Impartation Idea Inc., *Publishing Heaven's Heart*
Visit our website for online sales and contact information
AtWorkWithin.com

Copyright © 2016 by Rick Osborne (AtWorkWithin.com)

ISBN (softcover): 978-0-9950501-0-5   ISBN (EPUB): 978-0-9950501-1-2
ISBN (MOBI): 978-0-9950501-2-9

All rights reserved. No part of this book may be reproduced or transmitted in any form or by any means, electronic or mechanical, including photocopying and recording, or by any information storage and retrieval system, without permission in writing from the publisher.

(Church leaders who would like to photocopy small portions of this book for the purpose of internal church planning meetings may do so without permission.)

Unless otherwise noted, all scripture quotations are taken from the Holman Christian Standard Bible®. Used by permission HCSB © 1999, 2000, 2002, 2003, 2009 Holman Bible Publishers. Holman Christian Standard Bible®, Holman CSB®, and HCSB® are federally registered trademarks of Holman Bible Publishers.

The Holy Bible, English Standard Version® (ESV®) Copyright © 2001 by Crossway, a publishing ministry of Good News Publishers. All rights reserved.
Scripture quotations marked NLT are taken from the *Holy Bible*. New Living Translation copyright© 1996, 2004, 2007 by Tyndale House Foundation. Used by permission of Tyndale House Publishers, Inc. Carol Stream, Illinois 60188. All rights reserved.
Scripture taken from The Message. Copyright © 1993, 1994, 1995, 1996, 2000, 2001, 2002. Used by permission of NavPress Publishing Group.
Scripture quotations taken from the Amplified® Bible, Copyright © 2015 by The Lockman Foundation. Used by permission.
Scripture quotations marked NKJV are taken from the New King James Version®. Copyright © 1982 by Thomas Nelson, Inc. Used by permission. All rights reserved.
New Revised Standard Version Bible, copyright © 1989, Division of Christian Education of the National Council of the Churches of Christ in the United States of America. Used by permission. All rights reserved.

Underlining and bolding in scripture quotations reflect the author's added emphasis.

Cover design by Mark Herron (mrherronstudios@comcast.net)
Interior design and e-book formatting by Sun Editing & Book Design (suneditwrite.com)
Editing by Romana Osborne and Ed Strauss (inkwell_writing@yahoo.ca)

Printed and bound in Canada
2016—first edition

Special Sales: You can order multiple copies of this book to give away at our store on AtWorkWithin.com. To respond to our 1,000-book challenge please visit AtWorkWithin.com.

Library and Archives Canada Cataloguing in Publication

Osborne, Rick, 1961-, author
    At work within : be all that God created you to be / Rick Osborne.

Issued in print and electronic formats.
ISBN 978-0-9950501-0-5 (paperback).--ISBN 978-0-9950501-1-2 (epub).--ISBN 978-0-9950501-2-9 (mobi)

    1. Christian life. I. Title.

BV4501.3.O82 2016   248.4   C2016-901328-6
                                          C2016-901329-4

Table of Contents

A Word from the Author and Dedication 9

To Those Who Helped 11

Preface: A Word About Dreams 13

Introduction: Getting Started
Become the *you* God created you to be and live the wonderful life
that He intended. 15

The Seven Truths of Transformation:

Number 1 — In His Image
The goal of your salvation is transformation into His image. 21

Number 2 — His Disciples
Jesus wants to transform you personally by discipling you from within. ... 41

Number 3 — Righteousness and Grace
You can be transformed from within because Jesus gave you His
righteousness, and He empowers you. 59

Number 4 — From Faith to Faith
Everything you need to be transformed from within has been supplied,
but it won't happen by itself; you need to receive it and walk in it, by faith. ... 75

Number 5 — All Things New
Jesus redeemed everything about you, so that your transformation
could be successful and complete. 91

Number 6 — The Renewing of Your Mind
Having your mind renewed with God's Word is an essential part
of your transformation. 109

Number 7 — Transforming Prayer
Knowing what the Spirit taught about prayer through James, John,
and Paul will help you pray through your transformation. 127

Conclusion — Making Disciples
Getting back on track with the Great Commission 147

End Notes — Brainstorming with Church Leaders
Brainstorming and ideas to help you implement a disciple-making
program in your church. 179

A Word from the Author and Dedication

The most fun I've ever had reading a menu board was in a quaint little coffee shop where I began to literally laugh out loud when I read one menu item. Each line started with a description of the coffee and then gave its unique name so you could order it. Here's the one that got my attention:

Small, decaf, non-fat, no-whip latte....................... *"What's the Point?"*

I spent more than thirty years of my Christian life seeking and running after God with all my heart and strength, always wondering why I couldn't quite seem to get to where I wanted to be with God. I thought I was doing everything that good Christians were supposed to do, but I somehow knew that I was missing a key ingredient. Then something incredible happened: Jesus showed up and told me that He was going to start teaching me personally from His Word. He began to reveal things to me daily and guide me through the Bible like He was sitting next to me. In one short year I grew more in my understanding and closer to God than I had in the three decades prior; and it hasn't stopped.

In the process, I realized that I had never been taught clearly how to be a disciple of Jesus or taught the Gospel in its fullness, and consequently, I never truly and fully understood how to know God and grow in His grace.

Metaphorically speaking, the Gospel is like an extra-large, four shot, fully caffeinated, full-fat, extra-whip, extra-syrup mocha and I'd been surviving, ministering, and even thriving on a *"What's the Point"* latte for most of my Christian life.

This book is dedicated to my family, friends, and the many Christians I've met and/or attended church with along the way who have struggled in their relationship with God; who have—like me—wanted more of God, but always felt that something was missing. When Jesus came to me, at first I thought I was being treated in a special way. However, the first thing Jesus taught me is that He wants to teach all of us personally in the same way.

If you read this book with a seeking heart, in prayer, and with your Bible opened, ready to learn and grow, you and consequently your life, will be transformed far, far beyond "*What's the Point.*"

God loves you more than you can imagine and He's ready to help you see and wonderfully live "*The Point.*"

Enjoy your new life in Christ!

Rick Osborne

To Those Who Helped

Firstly, I want to thank my amazing wife Luba for
not only taking this transformation-by-grace journey with me,
but for also helping me with this book in so many ways,
from content to delivery and everything in between.
She's amazing!

I'd also like to thank those who read through the drafts of this book
and gave me encouragement, suggestions, corrections, and help:

Dr. Tom Blackaby
Dr. Todd Martin
George Bertness
Pastor Rob Scott
Ryan and Valerie Johnson
John and Rhonda Vanzuylekom

and also all those who were my guinea pigs in the first two
At Work Within courses who gave helpful comments on the first drafts.

And my wonderful editors Romana Osborne and Ed Strauss,
who helped me get the details right. To Mark Herron for his
cover design, and Jill Ronsley for her interior design.

Preface: A Word About Dreams

My Dream

I was holding a leather folder, packed full of correspondence and important papers, and I was standing near the bottom of a very large and majestic old stone staircase. I paused on the steps looking through the folder, fumbling and trying to find a certain piece of paper amongst the many. As I searched through the overstuffed and somewhat unorganized binder, I drew attention from those around me who crowded the ancient stairway. At first I was nonchalant about answering their questions and sharing that this was a folder full of correspondence and records between the King and myself. As more people gathered, I realized that my folder and my relationship with the King seemed quite a curiosity, and, to some, possibly scandalous or made-up. I began to feel nervous about the gathering crowd and became unwilling to reveal any more information. I closed my folder, looking to get away. One very calm onlooker stood a few steps away just smiling reassuringly at me; the smile told me it was okay. When I awoke I knew that God had spoken to me in a dream.

Over the years God has used dreams to get my attention. It's only fair to warn you that you're going to be reading about some of those dreams. And in preparation, I want to briefly clarify a few things: first of all, I share them reluctantly. I don't often share publicly what God shows me in private. However, if you haven't seen the connection yet, God used the dream above to show me that I was no longer to be nervous about sharing with others what He is doing in my life. In fact, I believe that God wants me to fill this book—the binder in the dream—with *what* and *how* He's taught me so that He can use it to encourage and help you.

Next, although God sometimes uses dreams to illustrate things, He uses the Bible as the foundation for what He teaches me, *not* dreams. Any dream that contradicts His Word, no matter how convincing or spectacular, should be given no more time than it takes you to shake it from your mind (Jeremiah 23:25–32; 1 Thessalonians 5:19–21). Although the Bible clearly tells you that God still speaks to His people in dreams (Acts 2:17), most dreams are just dreams (Ecclesiastes 5:3; Job 20:8; Isaiah 29:8).

When I prayerfully outlined this book I felt led to review the dreams God had given me and prompted me to write down. I was pleasantly surprised to see that God had given me a dream that would help illustrate each one of the biblical truths in this book; that's when I knew that the dreams had a larger purpose.

Each section of this book begins with one of those dreams. At the end of each section I use the dream's interpretation to help wrap up the section. I believe God did this more to enhance the book's creativity (and satisfy my need for illustrations) than to punctuate or enhance doctrine. So please, focus on the Bible verses that I teach from; read and study them. The experiences shared from my binder should merely inspire you to head up the ancient stone stairs for a visit of your own.

Introduction: Getting Started

Become the you God created you to be and live the wonderful life that He intended.

It's often said that a good teacher tells you what he/she is going to teach you, then teaches you, and finally tells you what you've just been taught. So I want to start by clearly telling you where I'm planning on taking you with this book.

In the Great Commission Jesus told you to "make disciples" for Him (Matthew 28:19). The Apostle Paul obeyed and taught converts how to be disciples of Jesus. The Bible tells you what and how he taught them and that's the basic foundation of this book. "The Seven Truths of Transformation" are the how-to of becoming a disciple of Jesus, and the conclusion of this book, "Making Disciples," looks at how the early church taught these truths and made disciples. The concluding section also discusses how we can do the same in our churches today.

Here are the book's eight sections expanded into a brief explanation of what you'll be learning.

In His Image

Truth Number 1: The goal of your salvation is transformation into His image.

Somewhere along the way we've gotten the idea that salvation is just about saying a prayer and getting a passport to heaven. It's *so* much more. God stated His original plan for each one of you when He said, "*Let Us make man in our image, according to our likeness*" (Genesis 1:26). In this section (Truth #1), I explain how God has never moved from this plan for you (even after Adam and Eve were sent from the Garden), and how Jesus made it possible for you to get back on track with being transformed into His image and likeness. I also teach how understanding what all this means—and how it works—can change you into the best *you* that you can be, the *you* God originally created you to be.

His Disciples

Truth Number 2: Jesus wants to transform you personally by discipling you from within.

In this section I show you what God's Word says about Jesus' personal *At Work Within* discipling program. I tell you how it works and how you can be loved, taught, led, and transformed by the Lord in a very real daily relationship. Jesus died for you so that you could be with Him, not just in the hereafter, but right now. I'll explain how what Jesus has provided for you, in the way of a relationship with Him, is even better than what the Twelve Disciples had when they walked with Him during His ministry here.

Righteousness and Grace

Truth Number 3: You can be transformed from within because Jesus gave you His righteousness and He empowers you by His grace.

Because of what Jesus did, when you received Him you were given the gift of His righteousness. God cleansed you, made you new, and declared you righteous by His grace when you received Jesus. However, God's purpose for grace did not change to "covering and/or excusing sin" once you were inside His Kingdom. The purpose of grace remains the same—it empowers change. Your salvation is complete but your transformation is ongoing and it's all by grace through faith. In this section I show you how the gift of righteousness and God's grace provide you with the foundation and the power to become all God intended you to be.

From Faith to Faith

Truth Number 4: Everything you need to be transformed from within has been supplied but it won't happen by itself; you need to receive it and walk in it by faith.

The Bible teaches that the just shall live by faith, that it's impossible to please God without faith and that you should not expect to receive any answers to your prayers without faith. Everything you receive from God is given to you by "grace through faith" (Ephesians 2:8) and, therefore, must be received by faith. So it's imperative that you understand what faith is and how it works. In this section I show you how to walk and grow in faith and how to use your faith to walk out your transformation.

All Things New
Truth Number 5: Jesus redeemed everything about you so that your transformation could be successful and complete.

The price Jesus paid for you is eternal; if it wasn't, eventually your salvation would end. In the same way, the price He paid for you was complete and for every part of you. If it wasn't, then only part of you would be welcomed into eternity and the parts of you that weren't saved would keep dragging you backwards. In this section I show you how your complete redemption sets you up to succeed in your relationship with God, your transformation, and in your life.

The Renewing of Your Mind
Truth Number 6: Having your mind renewed with God's Word is an essential part of your transformation.

The Bible teaches that God's people perish for lack of knowledge. God has given you the truth, promised to reveal it to you, teach it to you, write it on your heart, renew your mind with it, and cause your transformation—all by grace. It's an amazing, simple, and relational system that will have you running to God's Word excited about what Jesus will teach you next. In this section I'll explain how this works and get you started on the road to walking in the "mind of Christ" (1 Corinthians 2:16).

Transforming Prayer
Truth Number 7: Knowing what the Spirit taught about prayer through James, John, and Paul will help you pray through your transformation.

Jesus didn't do what He did just so your sins could be forgiven. Sin was the obstacle that needed to be obliterated so that God's purpose for you and His intended relationship with you could be realized. Jesus did all of what was necessary to demolish every obstacle and to transform you into His image—into mature sons and daughters of God who truly know Him, walk with Him, and become all He created you to be. All of that centers on an intimate and real relationship with the Father, the Son, and the Holy Spirit. Since the core and purpose of your redemption revolves around relationship, it's a given that understanding prayer is essential to your transformation. In this section I show you how your prayer life can be empowered by grace and facilitate your growth in relationship with God, the renewing of your mind, and your transformation into all God created you to be. When you discover prayer the way God intended it you won't want to stop.

Conclusion — Making Disciples
Getting back on track with the Great Commission

In this final section I show you how the early church turned the world upside-down by consistently turning new converts into real disciples of Jesus—disciples who knew how to fellowship with Him, receive His love, know Him, follow Him, learn from Him, carry on His work, and be transformed by Him. In this section I'll demonstrate how the "Seven Truths of Transformation" in this book were the foundation of what the early church taught to each new convert. The important question isn't, "How do revivals/renewals start?" it's "Why do they stop? I show you in this section that they stop because we stop making disciples.

So why is this book called *At Work Within*? Because that's how Jesus disciples you today and it's the key to your transformation. The *from-the-outside-in* discipleship program that the Jews in Jesus' day practiced was merely a metaphor or a shadow of the amazing *from-the-inside-out* discipleship program that Jesus, through His redemptive work and Holy Spirit, provided for each of you. Jesus told the Twelve that it would be better after He left physically, and it is. Now He can walk with you 24/7, teaching, leading, and transforming you from within. Enjoy the journey!

The Seven Truths of Transformation

In His Image

Truth Number 1

The goal of your salvation is transformation into His image.

My Dream

In my dream, I saw an easel and on it lay a large blank canvas ready for the artist's vision. God's hand held a brush and with one sure and precise stroke He was finished. It was an arching stroke—wide where the brush first touched, arching up, and then narrowing as the brush turned downward and was lifted from the canvas. I was puzzled. Why would God paint a painting with only one stroke? I walked closer to get a better look at God's handiwork. As I drew nearer, I began to see detail inside the stroke, then more detail, then even more. When I was next to the canvas, bent over slightly so that my face was looking down inside the stroke, I could see a cityscape, people, and many more details that went on forever. I was amazed. With one stroke and great ease, God had painted an impossibly beautiful, detailed, and perfect masterpiece.

When I woke up still marveling at the amazing painting—its image etched in my mind—the Father lovingly spoke, "That's your life, son."

For years my desire and daily prayer was, "Lord, I want to know You. I want to be all that You created me to be and accomplish all that You've called me to accomplish." I no longer pray that prayer and you'll understand why by the end of this section. My heart was right but I was missing the heart of the Gospel.

To be continued...

THE GOSPEL FOR CHRISTIANS

I believe that many Christians miss much of what their loving Heavenly Father has for them because somewhere along the way they started thinking that the Gospel is about receiving a free passport to heaven. It's so, so, so much more.

> So <u>I am eager to preach the good news to you also who are in Rome</u>. For I am not ashamed of the gospel, because it is God's power for salvation to everyone who believes… (Romans 1:15).

The verses in this chapter haven't changed since they were written close to 2,000 years ago but, like me for many years, you may have missed something each time you read them. Remember, Paul wrote this letter to *the church* in Rome (Romans 1:7) yet in verse 15 he said, "*I am eager to preach the good news to you also who are in Rome.*" Paul didn't say "to those who are in Rome" meaning the unsaved of Rome, he said "*to you*" meaning to those whom he was writing to, Christians. For many years I thought that the only ones who needed to hear the Gospel were people who had not yet received Jesus and perhaps those who needed to better understand what happened when they did.

In these verses, Paul explains that the Gospel is "*God's power for salvation to everyone who believes*"; not just when they first believe but also as they continue to believe. According to Paul, you are not just to enter God's Kingdom through the Gospel message, but you are to continue in the Gospel, living by the same faith in Jesus Christ that got you in.

Paul didn't have two messages; he preached the Gospel to the lost and continued to explain it to those who entered into it (Romans 16:25; Galatians 1:6–7; Philippians 1:27; Colossians 1:23; 2 Thessalonians 1:8). The Gospel is the Good News of God's Kingdom, not just the Good News about its entrance. Let's look at what else Paul wrote about this.

> For the word of the cross is folly to those who are perishing, <u>but to us who are being saved it is the power of God</u> (1 Corinthians 1:18 ESV).

In these verses Paul says that the message of the cross is for Christians who are "being saved." He says the same thing a little further on in this same letter.

> Now I would remind you, brothers, of the gospel I preached to you, which you received, in which you stand, <u>and by which you are being saved</u>... (1 Corinthians 15:1–2 ESV).

Although the thought might seem surprising at first, the Bible is clear that you are "*being saved*" by the Gospel. Now, just to be abundantly clear, the New Testament teaches that when you make a decision for Christ, you *are* saved.

> One believes with the heart, resulting in righteousness, and <u>one confesses with the mouth, resulting in salvation</u> (Romans 10:10; see also Ephesians 1:13; 2:4–5).

You *are* saved *and* you are *being* saved both by the Gospel, which is the power of God. The first is instantaneous and complete; the second is a process in which you progressively grow into what was already accomplished for you. Peter and James also wrote about "being saved."

> ... because <u>you are receiving the goal of your faith, the salvation of your souls</u> (1 Peter 1:9).

> Therefore, ridding yourselves of all moral filth and evil, <u>humbly receive the implanted word, which is able to save you</u> (James 1:21).

Paul also wrote about a future aspect of your salvation.

> Much more then, since we have now been declared righteous by His blood, <u>we will be saved through Him from wrath</u> (Romans 5:9; see also 1 Corinthians 3:15).

You *are* saved, you are *being* saved, and you *will be* saved. The Gospel is the Good News of God's love and what Jesus did for you, and it encompasses all three aspects of your salvation: past, present, and future. Paul wanted to go to Rome and preach the Gospel to the Christians there because he knew how important it was for them to understand, not just how to get into the Kingdom, but how to live and grow in the Kingdom.

You probably know what "getting saved" looks like and you can probably imagine that future moment when you'll enter the fullness of your salvation, but what does "being saved" look like? You'll need to back up to Genesis 1 to begin to answer that question.

THE HOPE OF GLORY

I was out for lunch with my pastor Rob. He had been preparing his sermon earlier and was pondering a question. After we ordered our lunch he sprang it on me. "How would you sum up the Gospel in seven words or less?" He still teases me about how I counted on my fingers as I quietly prayed and then spoke the answer, "*Let us make man in our image.*"

> Then God said, "Let Us make man in Our image, according to Our likeness" (Genesis 1:26).

Prior to this point in the creation story, the emphasis seemed to be on God the Father. In this verse, however, it's revealed that the plan to make humankind is something God the Father, God the Son, and God the Holy Spirit all agreed to do together. According to God's Word the decision to send Jesus to die for you was made before God said, "*Let there be light*" (1 Peter 1:20; Revelation 13:8). That means that God's "*Let Us*" conversation was not just talking about Adam being created with God-like attributes, but was prophetically looking forward to you being created new in Christ Jesus.

> For those He foreknew He also predestined to be conformed to the image of His Son ... (Romans 8:29).

God foreknew and predestined you to be conformed to the "*image of His Son.*" When did He foreknow and predestine this? When He said "*Let Us make man in Our image, according to Our likeness.*" Furthermore, the Bible tells you that Jesus *is* the image of the invisible God.

> He is the image of the invisible God, the firstborn over all creation (Colossians 1:15).

So when God said "*Let Us make man in Our Image*" He was talking about His plan to create you in Christ who *is* the image of God. This is a key thought! God knew that humankind would lose His image in the fall and He already planned for you to regain it and to fully realize it in Christ.

But why does Genesis 1:26 use both the words *image* and *likeness*? The word "*image*" seems to describe God's intent for you to have His nature and become Christlike, but what about the other word, "*likeness*"? If God meant "*likeness*" to show that His intent was for you to look like Him—two arms, two legs etc—that creates a problem; God the Father doesn't literally have a physical body and look like a man. But Jesus does!

> He (Jesus) emptied Himself by assuming the form of a slave, <u>taking on the likeness of men</u>. And when <u>He had come as a man in His external form</u>, He humbled Himself by becoming obedient to the point of death — even to death on a cross (Philippians 2:7–8).

Jesus was God's plan from the start and Genesis 1:26 prophetically looked forward to Jesus coming, being born as a man and taking on human likeness ("*taking on the likeness of men... as a man in His external form*"). God the Son, Jesus Christ, has two arms and two legs and He'll have His resurrected body forever. Jesus became like you so that you could be like Him (image and likeness). At the end of this age you will receive your glorified body which will be like Jesus' current heavenly body—and God's original and full intent for "*likeness*" will be completely realized.

> <u>He will transform the body of our humble condition into the likeness of His glorious body</u>, by the power that enables Him to subject everything to Himself (Philippians 3:21; see also 1 John 3:2).

God intended to fulfill His desire to make you in both His "*image and likeness*" by sending His Son. The Gospel was proclaimed in Genesis 1:26. The real important thing, however, is how that affects you today as you live your life as a Christian. Your body isn't junk that is somehow made special because God decided to live in you. Jesus designed your body (John 1:1–3) knowing He'd have one forever and that you'd be the temple of God's Spirit (1 Corinthians 6:19, 20): built by God, for God. In realizing this, you need to treat your body as much more than a disposable earth suit (1 Corinthians 3:16–17).

However, for the moment I'd like to focus on the image part, how that affects your everyday Christian life and what it shows you about the goal of "being saved." So let's look at some more New Testament passages.

Paul called the Gospel "*the gospel of the glory of Christ.*"

> In their case, the god of this age has blinded the minds of the unbelievers so they cannot see the light of <u>the gospel of the glory of Christ, who is the image of God</u> (2 Corinthians 4:4).

If the Gospel is *"the gospel of the glory of Christ"* what is *"the glory of Christ"*? Paul just said, *"the glory of Christ, who is the image of God"*; Jesus carried and displayed the image of God and that was His glory.

So what did Paul mean then when he taught that the glorious mystery of the Gospel is *"Christ in you, the hope of glory"*?

> God wanted to make known among the Gentiles the glorious wealth of this mystery, <u>which is Christ in you, the hope of glory</u>. We proclaim Him, warning and teaching everyone with all wisdom, <u>so that we may present everyone mature in Christ</u> (Colossians 1:27–28).

In your new birth you were created in His image and likeness. *"The hope of glory"* is the hope that you would carry and display Christ's image just as He carried and displayed the Father's image. The Gospel is *"the gospel of the glory of Christ"* because the Gospel proclaims that in Christ you realize God's original intention for you: *"Let Us make man in our image and likeness."*

Let's look at what Paul said to the Corinthians.

> We all, with unveiled face, <u>beholding the glory of the Lord</u>, are being transformed <u>into the same image</u> from one degree of glory to another (2 Corinthians 3:18 ESV).

Paul says that as you behold *"the glory of the Lord"* you are being transformed into *"the <u>same</u> image."* *"The glory of the Lord"* is the image of God. We are being transformed into what we are beholding: Jesus, who *is* the image of God, which is the glory of the Lord. Christ is in you by His Spirit to give you His life and transform you into His image—that's the Gospel of the glory of God, and God's original intent for mankind. Jesus' work on the cross did not just provide you with a passport to heaven. Jesus' work on the cross provided everything necessary to put you on the fast-track to His original intention for you.

> <u>His divine power has granted to us all things that pertain to life and godliness</u>, through the knowledge of him <u>who called us to his own glory and excellence</u>, by which he has granted to us his precious and very great promises, so that through them <u>you may become partakers of the divine nature</u>, having escaped from the corruption that is in the world because of sinful desire (2 Peter 1:3–4 ESV).

He has "*called us to His own glory and excellence*" and to be "*partakers of the divine nature.*" That's the image of God.

Believers are "*predestined to be conformed to the image of His Son*" (Romans 8:29). If you're a Christian, then that's been God's plan for you from the beginning of creation. And it's all provided for you in what Jesus did—you can't earn it or produce it in your strength. "*<u>His divine power has granted to us</u> all things that pertain to life and godliness…*" and "*<u>he has granted to us</u> his precious and very great promises, so that through them you may become partakers of the divine nature…*" Everything you need to be transformed into His image has been granted to you through God's promise and by His power.

Of course, that doesn't mean that you lose who you are and walk around in robes and sandals. No, in Christ you truly find who you are. It's mind-boggling to think that when God had that "*Let Us*" meeting, He looked ahead and saw each one of you living in Christ; unique sons and daughters of His, with eternal purpose, to be loved by Him and transformed into His image. To be Christlike means to become the individual son or daughter of God that He originally created you to be. Jesus is the firstborn and your example. God wants you to be like Jesus, following in His footsteps.

If you could get a glimpse of God's vision for you, who He's created you to be in Christ, it would absolutely overwhelm you. And your transformation into Christ's image and all God created you to be starts now, not when you're in heaven. You were born again with the purpose of growing up into Christ.

THE HOPE OF YOUR CALLING

So why aren't more Christians being radically transformed into the image of Christ? Mostly because they haven't been taught this part of the Gospel. Read these well-known verses in Ephesians:

> There is one body and one Spirit—just as you were <u>called to one hope at your calling</u>—one Lord, one faith, one baptism... (Ephesians 4:4–5).

Most of the basic Christian doctrines listed in these verses are understood by Christians. However, if you had asked me a few years ago what is the "*one hope*" that I'm called to, I probably would have said "heaven." That's not it. You don't need to be called to heaven. Paul explains elsewhere:

> ... God has chosen you <u>for salvation through sanctification by the Spirit and through belief in the truth. He called you to this through our gospel, so that you might obtain the glory of our Lord Jesus Christ</u> (2 Thessalonians 2:13–14).

You are called to sanctification (being saved) and the hope of that calling is that you "*might obtain the glory of our Lord Jesus Christ*" or be transformed into His image. Peter also talked about this:

> His divine power has granted to us all things that pertain to life and godliness, through the knowledge of him <u>who called us to his own glory and excellence</u>... (2 Peter 1:3 ESV).

He's "<u>*called*</u> *us to His own glory and excellence*" which is another way of saying, "He's called you to be transformed into His image," and getting there is the hope of that calling.

If you read all of the New Testament verses on what you're called to, you'll find that they all relate to being conformed to His image, called to be saints, called to live and suffer as He did, called into His marvelous light, called into holiness, called into fellowship with Jesus, called by grace, called according to His purpose, etc. The hope of your calling is the hope of being transformed into His image and truly growing up into all God created you to be.

In the above verses both Paul and Peter tell you that a prerequisite to transformation is knowing and believing the truth. Paul wrote, "*through sanctification by the Spirit and through belief in the truth*" and Peter wrote that He "*has granted to us all things that pertain to life and godliness, through the knowledge of him.*" How can you hope for something you don't know you've been called to? (See Romans 10:14–17.) When you simply believe that the hope of your calling is a passport to heaven, you live accordingly.

There are so many believers who are crying out for more of God but they don't know what they've been called to or how to walk in it. When those people learn, this world will change as they're transformed. If you're one of those people, or want to be one of those people, keep reading.

The next step is to start understanding how God accomplishes your transformation: when I first received my salvation, I got a mere glimpse and it changed my life. Back then, I had no idea that I had learned the first lesson in the mechanics of transformation.

AT WORK WITHIN

I freaked people out when I got saved (just shy of my nineteenth birthday). I was so changed, I hardly knew myself. People who knew me then still talk about the miraculous change that happened in me. God had radically changed me but now I had a different problem. I had just been saved, something that I had no understanding of, and I'd given my whole life to God, something I didn't even know people did and I didn't understand how to do. My heart, head, emotions, and desires were changed so much that most of the ways I thought, spoke, and acted prior to being saved, were now obsolete. I was definitely saved but in regards to my new life, I was very lost.

So not knowing what to do, whenever I heard something helpful about what "Christians were supposed to do," I just went and did it. I read every Christian book that anyone gave me or loaned to me. I heard that Christians were supposed to spend an hour a day in prayer so I spent two. I heard that I was supposed to read and underline my Bible so I spent all the time I used to spend partying doing that. I heard I was supposed to get baptized so I got baptized, etc, etc.

After a year of running around—with way more zeal than knowledge—doing my utmost to learn and be everything I could be for God, I was exhausted and inwardly failing. I had at that point either directly or indirectly led about a hundred people to the Lord. I spent one to three hours a day in prayer and Bible study. I had prayed for people and seen them healed. I ran a midweek Bible study and I was the unofficial youth leader of my church. However, in a quiet moment with the Lord, I realized that I was joyless and running on empty. God in His grace met me when I read these Bible verses.

> So then, my dear friends, just as you have always obeyed… work out your own salvation with fear and trembling. <u>For it is God who is working in you, enabling you both to desire and to work out His good purpose</u> (Philippians 2:12–13).

As I read I heard the Lord lovingly speak to me. He said, "It's not Rick at work within Rick." In a second, and by God's grace, I understood what God and His Word were saying. I had been running around trying to please God, earn His love and approval, *and make myself* into a perfect child of God.

Oh, I had been doing a ton of great things for God but "I" was doing them, running around Jesus like an overly-zealous but clueless puppy instead of learning to walk with Him and let Him transform me. I broke and wept for a long time. I realized then that God had committed to work within me and cause me to want to do, and to do, His good pleasure. Let's look at what God said through the prophet Ezekiel about the new birth.

> I will give you a new heart and put a new spirit within you; I will remove your heart of stone and give you a heart of flesh. I will place My Spirit within you <u>and cause you to follow My statutes and carefully observe My ordinances</u> (Ezekiel 36:26–27).

Read the last line again. God didn't just promise to make you new and put His Spirit in you; He promised that He'd *cause* you to follow and obey Him. Wow! That's exactly what Paul said. *"For God is working in you, giving you the desire to obey him, and the power to do what pleases him"* (Philippians 2:13 NLT). The Gospel, which was accomplished through Christ's work and given to you freely, includes both "getting saved" and walking out your salvation, that is, "being saved."

In order to get an even clearer picture of what Ezekiel was talking about, let's look at a parallel prophecy in Jeremiah.

> For this is the covenant that I will make with the house of Israel after those days, declares the LORD: <u>I will put my law within them, and I will write it on their hearts. And I will be their God, and they shall be my people</u> (Jeremiah 31:33 ESV).

Ezekiel said that God would give you a new heart and cause you to walk in His way. Jeremiah prophesied that God would write His law on your heart and the result would be that you would be His people, which meant that you would trust and obey Him. But in verse 31 of the same chapter, Jeremiah describes what the Holy Spirit was talking about: "*Behold, the days are coming, declares the LORD, when <u>I will make a **new covenant**</u> with the house of Israel and the house of Judah.*"

God clearly promised that through the New Covenant, He would secure your obedience—or cause you to walk in His way and be one of His faithful people.

In the verse before Jeremiah's prophecy about God putting His law within you, the Holy Spirit puts the promise in context.

> … <u>not like the covenant that I made with their fathers</u> on the day when I took them by the hand to bring them out of the land of Egypt, <u>my covenant that they broke</u>, though I was their husband, declares the LORD (Jeremiah 31:32 ESV).

What the Spirit is saying is that the Old Covenant didn't work because man kept breaking it—the Old didn't provide for humankind's obedience. So God proclaimed that the New Covenant would provide for your obedience. (See also Hebrews 10:15–18.)

God promised in Ezekiel 36:25–27, "*I will cleanse you,*" "*I will make you new,*" "*I will place my Spirit within you,*" and "*I will cause you to follow My statutes and carefully observe My ordinances.*"

Jesus shed His blood to pay the price for your sins, make you brand new, and bring you back to the Father. And God promised to work within you causing you to *want* to do, and to do, His good pleasure. In the New Covenant Jesus is not only the guarantor of our forgiveness and cleansing, He's the guarantor of our transformation (Hebrews 7:22).

The "at-work-within" revelation God gave me that day profoundly changed me, my relationship with God and my Christian walk. At that point I didn't understand the hope of my calling or the concept of "being saved," so I didn't realize that this truth was meant to progressively transform me into His image. However, whenever I felt I couldn't do something God wanted me to do I'd go to Him armed with Philippians 2:13 and He'd always work in me and pull me through. Once I realized that these Gospel promises were meant to facilitate my transformation into His image, I was again profoundly changed.

When God said, "*Let us make man in our image, and according to our likeness*," He had already devised a foolproof and complete plan to get you there and keep you there for all eternity. So far you've seen that you "are saved," that you're "being saved" and you will one day fully realize your salvation. The goal of your "being saved"—the hope of your calling—is to be transformed from glory to glory into Christ's image. Jesus didn't just die to secure your getting saved but also your "being saved." To facilitate your transformation, God made you new on the inside, placed His Spirit within you, and has promised to work in you and cause you to want to do (and actually do) His will—all so that you can be all God created you to be.

At this point you might ask, "What is the image of Christ? What does that look like?" Let's look at that next.

IN CHRIST

Jesus intentionally walked out His whole life knowing that He was the example of what we are to be transformed into.

Let's look at a few verses that talk about how you are to be like Him:

You have His mind; the same spiritual understanding, knowledge of God, attitude, and thoughts that Jesus did:

> Do nothing from selfish ambition or conceit, but in humility regard others as better than yourselves. Let each of you look not to your own interests, but to the interests of others. <u>Let the same mind be in you that was in Christ Jesus</u>... (Philippians 2:3–5 NRSV).

For who has known the Lord's mind, that he may instruct Him? <u>But we have the mind of Christ</u> (1 Corinthians 2:16; see also verses 12–15).

You are to love as He loved in thought, word, and deed:

This is how we have come to know love: He laid down His life for us. We should also lay down our lives for our brothers (1 John 3:16; see also John 15:12; 1 John 4:16–17).

You are to have the same unruffled, worry-free peace He had:

"Peace I leave with you. My peace I give to you. I do not give to you as the world gives. Your heart must not be troubled or fearful" (John 14:27).

You are to carry on His mission:

Jesus said to them again, "Peace to you! As the Father has sent Me, I also send you" (John 20:21; see also John 14:12).

You are to walk as He walked:

This is how we know we are in Him: <u>the one who says he remains in Him should walk just as He walked</u> (1 John 2:5–6).

You are to know, hear, and follow Jesus just as He knew, heard, and followed the Father:

"I am the good shepherd. <u>I know My own sheep, and they know Me, as the Father knows Me, and I know the Father</u>" (John 10:14–15; see also John 10:27).

You are to be righteous and holy as He was:

Little children, let no one deceive you! The one who does what is right is righteous, just as He is righteous (1 John 3:7).

But as the One who called you is holy, you also are to be holy in all your conduct; for it is written, Be holy, because I am holy (1 Peter 1:15–16).

You are to know, be empowered by, and be used by the Holy Spirit as Jesus was:

> You will receive power when the Holy Spirit has come on you, and you will be My witnesses in Jerusalem, in all Judea and Samaria, and to the ends of the earth (Acts 1:8; see also Acts 10:38).

To be transformed into the image of Christ is to progressively grow into having His attitude, His thoughts, His character, and God's love residing in you and flowing through you. It's growing to the place where you have God's Spirit active in your life and have the very mind of Christ (and, therefore, His wisdom and spiritual understanding); have His unmovable peace, do His works, and know and walk with Him as He knew and walked with the Father. It's walking like He walked as righteous children of God reflecting His glory in this world. It's knowing God and walking with Jesus in the power of the Holy Spirit. It's walking in the knowledge of the fact that you are "one spirit with God" (1 Corinthians 6:17) and becoming all God created you to be. Christians aren't called to just "know different," they're called to "be different"—to be amazing!

These few verses I've shared above only start to reveal who we are called to be in Christ. Now, here's a question for you: have you ever wondered, "If we're no longer under law, why are there are so many commands in the New Testament?" They're all there to show you what you're to become in Christ and what He's willing to do in you, not by law or self-effort, but by His promise and power.

Here's another question: have you ever thought about the utter impossibility of the "all" and "everything" requirements of the New Testament? Here are a few: Do *all* things without grumbling or disputing (Philippians 2:14). Rejoice *always*. Pray *without ceasing*. Give thanks in *all* circumstances (1 Thessalonians 5:16–18). Speak evil of *no one*. Show *perfect* courtesy to *all* people (Titus 3:2). *No* foul language is to come from your mouth, but *only* what is good… (Ephesians 4:29). Do not be anxious about *anything* (Philippians 4:6). Put away *all* malice and *all* deceit and hypocrisy and envy and *all* slander. Honor *everyone* (1 Peter 2:1, 17). Be holy in *all* your conduct (1 Peter 1:15).

If the writers of the New Testament had not understood the hope of your calling and the transforming power of His Spirit at work within you they wouldn't have raised the bar so high.

Do you know someone who is remarkably kind, so much so that everyone notices? How about remarkably generous? Patient? Wise? Loving? How about someone who has managed their God-given gifts well, grown in them, and excelled to remarkable heights? Have you ever marveled at someone who has an amazing relationship with God, is incredibly used by God, or someone who hears Him really well, or really understands the Bible and can wonderfully explain it? How about someone who has excelled in their calling in ministry, business, their career, the arts, etc?

These things and much more are *all* yours through Christ's work and the Spirit who works powerfully in you to transform you into His image. The person that God created you to be is probably beyond your imagining, but in Christ it's not beyond your reach.

NEW TESTAMENT EXAMPLES

Stephen was the first "not-one-of-the-twelve" guys transformed by becoming a post-Pentecost disciple of Jesus. The Bible says that he was full of faith and the Holy Spirit, full of grace and power, that he performed great wonders and signs among the people, and that his opponents couldn't stand against the wisdom and Spirit by which he spoke (Acts 6:5, 8). How long do you think Stephen had been a Christian when these things were written about him? Only around three years! Stephen was an ordinary guy—a deacon in the church—but he had been taught how to be Jesus' disciple and he knew the hope of his calling.

Can you imagine not only the impact on your own life but the impact on the world if all Christians were transformed like this? That impact is one of the things God had in mind when He devised His plan. Look at what He said through the prophet Ezekiel just before He spoke about making you new and causing you to obey.

> "I will honor the holiness of My great name ... The nations will know that I am Yahweh"—the declaration of the Lord God— "<u>when I demonstrate My holiness through you in their sight</u> (Ezekiel 36:23).

God said the nations will know that He is God when *He* demonstrates *His* holiness through you in their sight. He didn't say He'd demonstrate your best attempt at holiness. It's Him doing it in you and it's His holiness! Stephen was an early example of this. God changed him and demonstrated His glory and image through him.

We all think of the Apostle Paul as a superhero of the Faith, and he was, but we often miss why he was. In Philippians 3 Paul lists his pedigree, education, and accomplishments and then tells you that he counted all of that as rubbish so that he could be found in Christ. He said to the Corinthians:

> But by God's grace <u>I am what I am</u>, and His grace toward me was not ineffective. However, <u>I worked more than any of them</u>, yet not I, but God's grace that was with me (1 Corinthians 15:10).

Paul knew that all he became and all he did was because of Christ's work and the Spirit who was powerfully at work within him. The New Testament records Paul telling you to follow his example at least six times.

> Do what you have learned and received and heard and seen in me, and the God of peace will be with you (Philippians 4:9; see also 1 Corinthians 4:16; 11:1; Philippians 3:17; 1 Thessalonians 1:6; 2 Thessalonians 3:9).

Paul felt that he was an ordinary guy. In fact, because he persecuted the Church before he became a Christian, he saw his starting point as the worst of sinners. Paul believed that God used him to demonstrate how great the Gospel is at reaching and changing the worst people (1 Timothy 1:14–16). Paul was basically saying, "If God could save, transform, and use me, He can do it for anyone!" When you look to what you can accomplish in yourself, you have to set the standard really low so that you might hit it. But when you realize that you're predestined to be transformed into Christ's image by His promise, you see that Paul was God's example for you.

In the short time since I started trusting Him to work within me and transform me, I've grown more and gotten closer to Him than I did in the previous two decades. Letting Him be in charge of His transformation in me is incredibly freeing. He's not demanding that I perform but asking me to trust Him, and I'm always overwhelmed by His love and the changes He works in me. Change that I struggled with for years became simple in His hands.

Another great thing about my at-work-within transformation is that it's very normal and organic, if I can put it that way. I've realized that when a person tries to please God and change him or her self, the fruit is usually unnatural or hyper-religious. A seed reproduces itself; so only Jesus can produce His image in you; the fruit of your own efforts can only be a slightly-renovated you.

My dream continued…

In my dream that I recorded at the beginning of this section, Jesus was the brush in God's hand and my life was represented by God's one simple stroke. He showed me that my life is to be a masterpiece and that it's already been created, prepared, and promised in Christ Jesus. I just need to trust Him and walk in it, letting Him unfold it to my amazement—like when, in my dream, I walked up and admired what God had done.

The prayer I prayed in the first part of my Christian journey, "Lord, I want to know You. I want to be all that You created me to be and accomplish all that You've called me to accomplish," showed that I didn't understand the Gospel. I was struggling for what had already been given to me through the cross. Now I pray, "I thank You Father that I know You (Jeremiah 31:34) and I'm being transformed from glory to glory into Christ's image (2 Corinthians 3:18). I am Your creation created in Christ Jesus and I will do the good works that You prepared ahead for me to do (Ephesians 2:10)." There's a *big* difference between those two prayers! The first one left me wishing and struggling; the second leaves me trusting and resting in what God has already accomplished and promised to do within me.

No matter who you are, what you've been through, what you've done, or what obstacles are in your way, He will forgive you, transform you, and make your life beautiful in Christ Jesus. Talk to Him and start your at-work-within transformation journey now.

What God taught me about transformation has been life-changing. However, the next transformation truth has done more to wonderfully change me and my relationship with God than anything else. When I first became a Christian I didn't know what to do; I was running all over the place trying to give my life to God and do what He wanted me to do. Unfortunately, no one showed me how to be Jesus' disciple, how to walk with Him, learn from Him, and be transformed by Him.

POWER POINTS FROM TRUTH NUMBER 1
Quotes for Sharing on Social Media

*The Gospel is the Good News of God's Kingdom,
not just the Good News about its entrance.*

∽

*When God said, "Let Us make man in Our Image," He was
talking about His plan to create you in Christ who is the image of God.*

∽

*You are saved and you are being saved both
by the Gospel, which is the power of God.*

∽

*Jesus became like you so that you could
be like Him (image and likeness).*

∽

*Jesus designed your body knowing He'd have one forever and that
you'd be the temple of God's Spirit, built by God, for God.*

∽

Jesus carried and displayed the image of God and that was His glory.

∽

*Everything you need to be transformed into His image has been
granted to you through God's promise and by His power.*

∽

*Jesus is the firstborn and your example.
God wants you to be like Jesus, following in His footsteps.*

The hope of your calling is the hope of being transformed into His image and truly growing up into all God created you to be.

Jesus is not only the guarantor of our forgiveness and cleansing, He's the guarantor of our transformation (Hebrews 7:22).

∾

The goal of your "being saved"–the hope of your calling– is to be transformed from glory to glory into Christ's image.

∾

Jesus intentionally walked out His whole life knowing that He was the example of what we are to be transformed into.

∾

You are to know, hear, and follow Jesus just as He knew, heard, and followed the Father.

∾

Christians aren't called to just "know different," they're called to "be different"–to be amazing!

∾

The person that God created you to be is probably beyond your imagining, but in Christ it's not beyond your reach.

∾

Paul knew that all he became and all he did was because of Christ's work and the Spirit who was powerfully at work within him.

∾

Only Jesus can produce His image in you; the fruit of your own efforts can only be a slightly-renovated you.

His Disciples

Truth Number 2

Jesus wants to transform you personally
by discipling you from within.

My Dream

I dreamed that a small group of us who somehow worked together, were meeting in a warehouse to discuss what was going on where we worked and see how we could make things better. We had just all arrived and one of my co-workers announced that Jesus would be meeting us there. I said that perhaps he should use the word "appearing" because the word "meeting" made it sound like Jesus would be attending bodily. I explained that although Jesus can appear to us in many ways (Acts 9:3–5, 10; 18:9; 23:11), that He would not return bodily until the Second Coming.

While I was busy pontificating about what Jesus would and wouldn't do He appeared in person in the center of our little group. Now, I'm not sure how Jesus shows up personally in a dream, but I think I derailed the process with my response. He was smiling at me and His face and expression were filled with so much love and joy. In that instant, when I realized it was actually Jesus, I leaped and wrapped my arms around His neck. I was giddy with excitement and joy, acting like a little child reunited with one of his parents. He took the momentum of my jump, like a father would a child, and swung me half a turn around the circle and put me down, still smiling at me.

I woke up full of wonder. I could remember exactly what He looked like. His amazing loving face is still etched in my mind.

In John 14:21 Jesus said, "*I also will love him and reveal Myself to him.*"

To be continued...

JESUS WITH US

"The Great Commission" gives you something to do and something you must *remember* while you're doing it. Jesus commanded:

> "Go, therefore, and make disciples of all nations, baptizing them in the name of the Father and of the Son and of the Holy Spirit, teaching them to observe everything I have commanded you. And <u>remember, I am with you always, to the end of the age</u>" (Matthew 28:19–20).

The Greek word translated "remember" in verse 20 is *idou*. There isn't a word in the English language that can be used to translate it adequately. It means, "listen to this, pay close attention, understand," but with great emphasis. Today, in casual writing, you use underlining, bolding and/or exclamation marks to draw your reader's attention in the same way that using this Greek word was meant to flag something. So this might be a reasonable modern-day rendering of the one word, "<u>Pay attention! Listen! Understand! Hey, this is **IMPORTANT!!!**</u>" Jesus wanted you to pay really close attention to this simple statement: "*I am with you always, to the end of the age.*"

Why is that so **IMPORTANT**? It's vital because we were never meant to be disciples of an absentee Master.

Many of you are familiar with the time Jesus appeared to Paul and knocked him to the ground (Acts 9:3–6). But what we don't often hear about is that Paul continued experiencing Jesus personally but in a much more encouraging way.

> Then <u>the Lord said to Paul in a night vision</u>, "Don't be afraid, but keep on speaking and don't be silent. <u>For I am with you</u>, and no one will lay a hand on you to hurt you, because I have many people in this city" (Acts 18:9–10).

> "After I came back to Jerusalem and was praying in the temple complex, I went into a visionary state <u>and saw Him telling me</u>, 'Hurry and get out of Jerusalem quickly, because they will not accept your testimony about Me!'" (Acts 22:17–18).

The following night, <u>the Lord stood by him and said</u>, "Have courage! For as you have testified about Me in Jerusalem, so you must also testify in Rome" (Acts 23:11).

For I would have you know, brothers, that the gospel that was preached by me is not man's gospel. For I did not receive it from any man, nor was I taught it, <u>but I received it through a revelation of Jesus Christ</u> (Galatians 1:11–12).

<u>But the Lord stood with me and strengthened me</u>, so that the proclamation might be fully made through me and all the Gentiles might hear. So I was rescued from the lion's mouth (2 Timothy 4:17).

The Bible records Paul receiving direction from God through angels (Acts 27:23–24), through fellow believers (Acts 13:2; 20:23; 21:4, 11), and directly from the Holy Spirit (Acts 13:9; 16:6–10). However, out of all the ways that God used to direct Paul, the one that is recorded the most is through Jesus personally.

In case you're wondering, this type of experience was not just for Paul the Apostle. Jesus said that He'd reveal Himself to those who love Him (John 14:21). Here's what happened to a regular non-apostolic disciple:

There was a disciple in Damascus named Ananias. And <u>the Lord said to him in a vision</u>, "Ananias!" "Here I am, Lord!" he said (Acts 9:10).

One thing that I find wonderful about these reports in Scripture is that the people who experienced Jesus in this way, and/or recorded the experiences, didn't act and/or write like these experiences were out of the ordinary. Of course Jesus revealing Himself to you is just a small part of what He means when He says, *"And remember, I am with you always, to the end of the age,"* but these stories illustrate just how real your relationship with Him can be.

The part of the Great Commission that Mark recorded ended with a report of what happened after Jesus ascended and the Holy Spirit came.

Then after speaking to them, the Lord Jesus was taken up into heaven and sat down at the right hand of God. And they went out and preached everywhere, <u>the Lord working with them and confirming the word by the accompanying signs</u> (Mark 16:19–20).

Jesus sat down at the right hand of the Father but was also with His disciples working with them. The Greek word translated *"working with them"* means "to be a co-worker."

The whole reason why Jesus told His disciples that He'd always be with them is so that you would *understand* and *remember* that the discipleship program was never meant to end, only change.

DISCIPLESHIP TRANSITION

In Jesus' time, being someone's disciple was a full-time occupation. Disciples left their jobs and went to be trained under their master (Matthew 4:20, 22; 19:27), often going and living with the master (John 1:38–39), to serve and learn from him. Eventually, the disciple was fully trained and either worked on their own in what they learned from the master or they took over the master's place of honor; it was a serious lifelong commitment on behalf of the master and the disciple. That's why Jesus' Disciples were so concerned when, after only a few short years, Jesus told them that He was going away.

> Jesus knew they wanted to question Him, so He said to them, "Are you asking one another about what I said, 'A little while and you will not see Me; again a little while and you will see Me'? I assure you: You will weep and wail, but the world will rejoice. You will become sorrowful, but your sorrow will turn to joy" (John 16:19–20).

As Jesus got closer to the cross He knew that He needed to explain the coming change to His Disciples. Part of that explanation is found in the "Final Discourse" which starts at the end of John 13 and finishes at the end of John 17. Jesus starts the conversation—and sets the context—in John 13:33 by addressing His Disciples as *"children."* The Greek word used there is a term that masters used when addressing their disciples.

Jesus then tells them He's going away and begins to explain the transition and future of their discipleship program. Let's look at some verses that specifically deal with the discipleship issue.

"I will not leave you as orphans; <u>I am coming to you</u>" (John 14:18).

Jesus began the conversation in John 13:33 by calling His Disciples "*children*" referring to their position as His disciples. He refers to that position again by using the word "*orphan.*" Jesus is telling them that even though change is coming that He will continue being their Master.

> "Your heart must not be troubled. Believe in God; believe also in me. In my Father's house are many dwelling places; if not, I would have told you. I am going away to prepare a place for you" (John 14:1–2).

Jesus was telling His Disciples that He was going away but He assured them that they didn't need to be troubled. Then He confirmed their ongoing place as His Disciples by talking to them about living with Him. Remember, disciples were supposed to live with their masters. So Jesus told them that they'd be living with Him in His Father's house. I'm not diminishing the fact that Jesus has prepared a future place in God's heavenly house for us; but Jesus was also telling His Disciples that—starting shortly—they'd have a permanent place in God's house as part of God's family and therefore would be dwelling with Jesus as His Disciples forever.

A little further on in His discussion with His Disciples, Jesus again used the same word that He used for "*house*" in verse one.

> Judas (not Iscariot) said to Him, "Lord, how is it You're going to reveal Yourself to us and not to the world?" Jesus answered, "If anyone loves Me, he will keep My word. My Father will love him, and <u>We will come to him and make Our **home** with him</u>" (John 14:22–23).

The Disciples were trying to understand how Jesus could go away but continue to be their Master without anyone else seeing Him. Jesus told them that they would be part of God's family, living in God's house and that He and the Father were going to come and make their "*home*" with them. Jesus was telling them that the way He discipled them was about to change. It would be no less real and constant—in fact, it would be more so; they were about to become the temple of the Holy Spirit and Jesus would be disciplining them from the inside-out.

INSIDE-OUT DISCIPLESHIP

Christians often think about how great it would have been to walk with Jesus as one of the Twelve. However, while Jesus was preparing the Disciples for the transition He said that it would be better to be His disciple *after* He ascended.

> "It is for your benefit that I go away, because if I don't go away the Counselor will not come to you. If I go, I will send Him to you" (John 16:7).

The Twelve were actually a type or picture of what was to come. God chose the concept of Jewish discipleship as a metaphor for what He intended from the start. Jesus' goal was to go to the cross and make a way for billions to be discipled by Him personally and individually. So He chose Twelve to train from the outside-in, and then He moved them from that to being discipled from the inside-out so that hopefully they'd get the picture.

God used discipleship as a metaphor to show how His original plan for us—*"Let Us make man in our image"*—would be realized. Jesus has guaranteed through His redemptive work that you will be transformed into His image and walk in God's will and plan for your life. A big part of how He does that is by walking with you and discipling you from within. Just like a disciple in Jesus' day was to walk closely with His master 24/7 and become exactly like him, so you are to truly walk with Jesus and be transformed into His image through the indwelling of His Spirit.

There's one amazing statement that Jesus made that I think sums up what He taught about your relationship with Him and what it would look like. If you can simply believe what Jesus says here and trust Him to work it in you, your life will be changed.

> "I know my own sheep, and they know me, just as my Father knows me and I know the Father" (John 10:14–15 NLT).

Jesus laid down His life, not just to rescue you, but also so He could have a relationship with you like He had with the Father. <u>*Remember!*</u>

Before Jesus went to the cross, the intimate Master/disciple relationship that He had with Peter, James, and John was only a taste of what was to come. Your relationship with Jesus is meant to be a growing, loving, very real, and eternal relationship with your Lord and Master who wants to walk with you, talk with you, reveal Himself to you, teach you, bless you, and see you transformed into His image.

Take a few minutes now to talk with the Lord about the relationship you want with Him. Remember, He made you for intimate relationship with Him, He paid the price to restore it, and He desires it more than you can imagine.

TAUGHT BY THE LORD

On November 10, 2010 Jesus revealed Himself to me. In just a few amazing moments He very simply told me that He was going to start teaching me personally from His Word. Well, He did in a very real way, and that's when my journey that led to this book began. At first I felt very special to have been selected for this; but then He taught me that He has promised to teach each and every Christian in the same personal way. Turns out that I *am* special, just like every other disciple of Jesus.

Let's look closer at what the Bible has to say.

After Jesus rose from the dead He appeared to two of His disciples on the Road to Emmaus (Luke 24:13–35). Jesus prevented His two disciples from recognizing Him at first and explained to them what the scriptures said about the Messiah (Luke 24:27). At the end of the conversation Jesus revealed who He was and then immediately disappeared. Here's what they said as soon as He vanished:

> So they said to each other, "Weren't our hearts ablaze within us while He was talking with us on the road and explaining the Scriptures to us?" (Luke 24:32).

The two disciples said that their hearts were "ablaze" or "set on fire." They were listening with their ears but Jesus was showing them what it felt like to hear Him with their hearts, know the truth, and get excited about His Word. When Jesus started teaching me I experienced this and

I still do; as I'm searching His Word, meditating on it and asking Him questions, suddenly verses and concepts come together and I get it! When that happens there's a knowing and an excitement inside me that I would also describe as my heart being "set on fire."

That same evening Jesus appeared to more of His disciples and opened their minds to understand the scripture as well.

> Then He told them, "These are My words that I spoke to you while I was still with you—that everything written about Me in the Law of Moses, the Prophets, and the Psalms must be fulfilled." <u>Then He opened their minds to understand the Scriptures</u> (Luke 24:44–45).

Before Jesus' death and resurrection, it's not recorded that He did this even once for His Disciples. To the contrary, the Disciples often didn't understand what Jesus taught and it seems that they blamed Jesus for not "*speaking plainly.*"

> "Ah!" His disciples said. "Now You're speaking plainly and not using any figurative language" (John 16:29).

Jesus knew that only after He had redeemed His disciples and come to them through the Holy Spirit, could He really start teaching them. Here's what Jesus said as He was preparing them for inside-out discipleship:

> "<u>I still have many things to tell you, but you can't bear them now</u>. When the Spirit of truth comes, <u>He will guide you into all the truth</u>" (John 16:12–13).

> "I have spoken these things to you in figures of speech. <u>A time is coming when I will no longer speak to you in figures, but I will tell you plainly about the Father</u>" (John 16:25).

Jesus knew that once they were made new and indwelt by the Holy Spirit, that all of His disciples—including you—could be taught and caused to bear (hear, understand, and live) the things of God. And Jesus promised that He, Himself, would teach you and speak to you plainly about the Father.

It was always part of God's plan to teach you from within. The Prophets predicted it, Jesus told His Disciples it was coming, and the New Testament writers wrote about it. Jeremiah's prophecy about the New Covenant talked about the way disciples would learn.

> "This is the covenant I will make with the house of Israel after those days... <u>I will put My teaching within them and write it on their hearts</u>. I will be their God, and they will be My people" (Jeremiah 31:33).

God declares that in the New Covenant He'll be within each believer, revealing Himself to you, and teaching you individually. The statement "*I will put my teaching within them*" is basically saying, "I will instruct them from within." In the previous verse God said that He took the Israelites "*by the hand.*" The Holy Spirit was intentionally contrasting the Israelite's "outside-in" relationship with the coming "inside-out" relationship in Christ. Notice the phrase "*<u>and write it on their hearts</u>.*" Jesus teaches you His Word from within, then He writes it on your heart, or causes you to understand it and live it (Philippians 2:13). When Jesus teaches you something, it comes packed with all the power it needs to have it sink in and transform you.

Isaiah 54 is an amazing chapter prophesying about the New Covenant. Paul quotes and teaches from it in Galatians 4, and Jesus quoted from it as well.

> Then all your children will be taught by the LORD, their prosperity will be great, and you will be established on a foundation of righteousness (Isaiah 54:13–14).

> It is written in the Prophets: <u>And they will all be taught by God</u>. Everyone who has listened to and learned from the Father comes to Me... (John 6:45).

I like the way the Amplified Version brings out the meaning of what Jesus said: "*And they shall all be taught by God—have Him in person for their teacher...*"

Jesus is your Teacher and He has promised to teach you personally through His Spirit who dwells in you (John 14:20; 16:13–15). Jesus said

He wouldn't leave you as an orphan—a disciple without a master—He comes to you by His Spirit as your Master and Teacher to disciple you from within.

Paul wrote that he was taught the Gospel by the Lord Himself (Galatians 1:12), and we tend to think that he was a special case, but that's not entirely true, nor is it what he taught in his letters.

> As it is written: "What eye did not see, and ear did not hear, and what never enter the human mind—God prepared this for those who love him." Now <u>God has revealed these things to us by the Spirit</u>, for the Spirit searches everything, even the depths of God… Now <u>we have not received the spirit of the world, but the Spirit who comes from God, so that we may understand what has been freely given to us by God</u> (1 Corinthians 2:9–10, 12).
>
> I pray that the God of our Lord Jesus Christ, the glorious Father, <u>would give you a spirit of wisdom and revelation in the knowledge of Him</u> (Ephesians 1:17; see also 1:7–8).

Paul didn't just write about concepts, he also wrote conversationally about being taught by God. If the above verses seem a little lofty, the ones below give simple examples of what He was talking about.

> Therefore, all who are mature should think this way. <u>And if you think differently about anything, God will reveal this to you also</u> (Philippians 3:15).
>
> About brotherly love: you don't need me to write you because <u>you yourselves are taught by God to love one another</u> (1 Thessalonians 4:9).
>
> Consider what I say, for <u>the Lord will give you understanding in everything</u> (2 Timothy 2:7).

Paul believed that God would "*reveal*" truth to believers, that you are "*taught by God*," and that the Lord would give you "*understanding in everything*." This matches perfectly with what He said in the more lofty-sounding verses: that the Spirit reveals to you "*the things that were freely given to us by God*", that Jesus gives you "*all wisdom and understanding*" and that God wants to give you "*a spirit of wisdom and revelation in the knowledge of Him.*" Notice how wonderfully involved the Father, Son, and Holy Spirit are in the promise and how committed they are to teaching you "*Let Us make…*"

The next question is: How do you cooperate with the process and learn from Him?

LEARNING FROM HIM

Jesus gave some insight into what you need to do to grow in receiving His teaching.

> At that time Jesus said, "I praise You, Father, Lord of heaven and earth, because <u>You have hidden these things from the wise and learned and revealed them to infants</u>. Yes, Father, because this was Your good pleasure. <u>All things have been entrusted to Me by My Father</u>. No one knows the Son except the Father, <u>and no one knows the Father except the Son and anyone to whom the Son desires to reveal Him</u>. "Come to Me, all of you who are weary and burdened, and <u>I will give you rest</u>. All of you, take up My yoke <u>and learn from Me</u>, because I am gentle and humble in heart, and you will find rest for yourselves. For My yoke is easy and My burden is light" (Matthew 11:25–30).

Jesus thanked the Father that truth is hidden from those who are wise and learned in this world, and revealed to infants. The word "*infant*" should remind you of when Jesus called His Disciples "*children*" (John 13:33), the verse from Isaiah ("*all your <u>children</u> will be taught of the LORD*"), and Jesus' reference to not leaving you as "*orphans*" (John 14:18). Jesus isn't comparing children to wise people. Jesus is talking about us—those who have become God's disciples.

Where did God hide His truth? In Christ. "*All the treasures of wisdom and knowledge are hidden in Him*" (Colossians 2:3). Why? Hiding the truth was necessary because without the Teacher inside you, you can't bear what God wants to teach you. However, once you're in Christ, God takes great pleasure in revealing Himself and His will to you.

Jesus said, "*No one knows the Father except the Son and anyone to whom the Son desires to reveal Him*" (Matthew 11:27). So how do you get Jesus to reveal to you what God wants you to know? That's the easy part because Jesus tells you, "*Come to Me… Take up My yoke <u>and learn from Me</u>.*" You need to "*come*" to Him and let Him to teach you; a good teacher knows that He can only teach those who want to learn.

A yoke is a farming implement used to connect two animals together so that they can pull a plow in unison. Jesus uses this picture to show how the learning works. Whether you're praying and reading your Bible, loving your family, or at work, you're to *remember* that you're walking with your Master and trust Him to teach and transform you moment by moment. When I feel that I'm struggling or not walking in step with Him, I stop what I'm doing, acknowledge His presence, and ask Him to teach me.

I used to struggle to read my Bible thinking that only with far more intelligence than I believed I possessed, could I really understand it. Now I trust the Author who is in me, to teach me and I can't wait to open my Bible and spend time with Jesus learning. When you read and study the Bible knowing the Teacher is in you, lovingly teaching you, you'll have trouble putting it down.

Let's look at another place where Jesus teaches about learning from Him.

> He taught them many things in parables, and in His teaching He said to them: "<u>Listen! Consider the sower who went out to sow</u>…." Then He said, "<u>Anyone who has ears to hear should listen!</u>" <u>When He was alone with the Twelve, those who were around Him asked Him about the parables.</u> He answered them, "<u>The secret of the kingdom of God has been given to you</u>…" (Mark 4:2, 3, 9–12).

Notice the first word and the last phrase that Jesus spoke when telling this parable: "*Listen!*" and "*Anyone who has ears to hear should listen!*" The word "*listen*" here means to "pay attention, understand and hearken, or act on what you learn." Jesus was speaking to a large crowd and before

He started, and after He finished, He let them all know that they needed to pay attention and get this. And yet, when Jesus finished telling the parable, no one understood it. How do I know that? When the Disciples came and asked Jesus what the parable meant, He told them that it was given to them to understand, but that everyone else just heard a parable. So the rest of the crowd went away without understanding. The Disciples didn't understand either because they had to ask Jesus what it meant. So no one understood.

So what separated the crowd from the Disciples and how did they end up understanding? They did something very simple: they went to Jesus, trusted Him to teach them, and asked Him what it meant. Jesus said, *"Do you not understand this parable? How then will you understand any of the parables?"* (vs. 13) Jesus taught that the secret to understanding anything about God is to go to Him and trust Him to teach you.

In verse 8 Jesus talked about seed that fell on good ground and produced a crop from the seed, 30, 60, and 100 times what was sown. That's a miraculous yield for any crop. When you trust Jesus to teach you, His Word can produce more transformation in your life than you can imagine. Jesus is the Sower. He's with you to sow the Word in your heart, teach you, and produce a huge crop in you.

When you read and study the Bible, slow down and talk with your Master, rest and trust Him to teach you. Be patient with the process and keep trusting Him. As with most things you'll need to walk before you run.

So, if the Lord is the One who teaches you, where do Bible teachers fit into the picture?

WHAT ABOUT TEACHERS?

Let's look at what the Apostle John had to say about teachers and learning from God.

> I have written these things to you about those who are trying to deceive you. The anointing you received from Him remains in you, <u>and you don't need anyone to teach you</u>. Instead, <u>His anointing teaches you about all things</u>, and is true and is not a lie; just as He has taught you, remain in Him (1 John 2:26–27).

John wrote this letter to *teach* believers (1 John 5:13), so to think he's teaching that teachers are unnecessary would be a contradiction. In context, John was dealing with false teachers, "*those who are trying to deceive you.*" The phrase, "*you don't need anyone to teach you*" can be understood to be saying, you don't need *a certain person or specific teacher* to teach you. John knew that when you get your eyes on teachers instead of the Teacher that you can be led astray. No teacher should ever occupy Jesus' position as your Teacher.

God has given teachers in the Body. However, when you don't realize that you're Jesus' disciple, not man's, then you mistakenly start to rely on teachers and accept what they say unquestioningly. Even the apostle Paul told his listeners, "*Judge for yourselves what I say*" (1 Corinthians 10:15). When you follow people you leave yourself open to being deceived because you've put them in Christ's place. Notice that the Apostle John didn't tell his readers to listen to him instead of listening to others. He sent them to the Teacher. John remembered that Jesus had called Him to make disciples for Jesus, not for himself, and he was reminding his readers whose disciples they were.

Jesus said, "*... you have one Teacher, and you are all brothers*" (Matthew 23:8); and Paul rebuked the Corinthians for focusing on certain teachers (1 Corinthians 1:11–13).

Paul went into many cities and towns to proclaim the Gospel. In each city some rejected him and some listened, but the response of the Jews of Berea stands out.

> The Jews received Paul's message with enthusiasm and met with him daily, <u>examining the Scriptures to see if they supported what he said</u>... (Acts 17:11 MSG).

The Jews of Berea had no trouble receiving Paul's message with enthusiasm because they didn't rely on him as their teacher; instead, they examined the scripture. Today you need to be careful that you don't automatically believe a teacher and accept what he says because he's a persuasive speaker or because he's part of your group. You also need to be careful to not reject a Bible teacher and all that he says because he's not part of your group. Your group is not your Teacher.

You need to trust the Lord to teach you and keep your Bible handy, open, and well-used. The fact is, no Bible teacher has all the truth and you're never to unthinkingly follow teachers; you follow Jesus. The goal of great Bible teachers—like Paul and John—is to help you be a disciple of *the* Teacher. Whether 12 or billions, one thing has never changed—you are to be Jesus' disciple and to make disciples for *Him* (Acts 9:1, 10, 36; 16:1; 21:16).

Remember though, just because you have His promise to teach you doesn't mean you'll know everything overnight. Be humble and listen to teachers while trusting and listening to Him; and let others teach you how to study His Word and how to be Jesus' disciple. Jesus gave the Church the task of making disciples for Him, so let others help you; and, like the Jews of Berea, always be open to change what you believe when you see the truth in God's Word.

There are three common ways to fall into error: (1) find teachers (or a church) you trust and believe everything they teach without studying for yourself and being taught by Him; (2) discard all teachers thinking you only need Jesus; (3) or discard diligent study in the Word because you think Jesus will just tell you everything Himself without requiring any effort on your part.

My dream continued…

At the beginning of this section I talked about how Jesus manifested Himself to me in a dream. That kind of experience is amazing and you can expect Jesus to manifest Himself to you in many different ways; however, *remember*, Jesus is walking with you and teaching you, whether it always feels like He is or not; *"the righteous shall live by faith"* (Romans 1:17). I woke up from the dream and Jesus was still with me—even though I couldn't see Him—and the more I believe that, the more I end up actually experiencing Him. Christianity is a very real relationship with Jesus your Master, Lord, Teacher, and Guide.

Summing things up so far: It's always been God's plan to create His children in His image and likeness in Christ Jesus. Your salvation not only includes getting saved but *being* saved—being progressively transformed into the image of Jesus by His promise and power. Jesus walks with you 24/7 in a real relationship, discipling you and working within you. People like Paul, Stephen, and Philip are examples of what God can do in and through you as you learn from Jesus and are transformed.

Stop and talk to Him now about your desire to walk with Him and be taught by Him.

Next let's look at righteousness and grace and the part they play in your being His disciple and being transformed into His image.

POWER POINTS FROM TRUTH NUMBER 2
Quotes for Sharing on Social Media

Jesus wanted you to pay really close attention to this simple statement: "I am with you always, to the end of the age."

∽

We were never meant to be disciples of an absentee Master.

∽

Out of all the ways that God used to direct Paul, the one that is recorded the most is through Jesus personally.

∽

Jesus' goal was to go to the cross and make a way for billions to be discipled by Him personally and individually.

∽

God used discipleship as a metaphor to show how His original plan for us—"Let Us make man in our image"—would be realized.

∽

Jesus laid down His life, not just to rescue you, but also so He could have a relationship with you like He had with the Father.

∽

Jesus promised that He, Himself, would teach you and speak to you plainly about the Father.

Jesus teaches you His Word from within, then He writes it on your heart, or causes you to understand it and live it.

∼

Jesus is your Teacher and He has promised to teach you personally through His Spirit who dwells in you.

∼

When you read and study the Bible knowing the Teacher is in you, lovingly teaching you, you'll have trouble putting it down.

∼

Jesus is the Sower. He's with you to sow the Word in your heart, teach you, and produce a huge crop in you.

∼

When you read and study the Bible, slow down and talk with your Master, rest and trust Him to teach you.

∼

No teacher should ever occupy Jesus' position as your Teacher.

∼

The Apostle John didn't tell his readers to listen to him instead of listening to others. He sent them to the Teacher.

∼

No Bible teacher has all the truth and you're never to unthinkingly follow teachers; you follow Jesus.

∼

Whether 12 or billions, one thing has never changed–you are to be Jesus' disciple and to make disciples for Him.

Jesus gave the Church the task of making disciples for Him, so let others help you.

∽

Jesus is walking with you and teaching you, whether it always feels like He is or not; "the righteous shall live by faith."

Righteousness and Grace

Truth Number 3

You can be transformed from within because Jesus gave you His righteousness and He empowers you by His grace.

My Dream

I was standing in a backyard with someone who at first, I thought was my dad. We both stood there casually watching his dog play. I noticed that the dog was incredibly well behaved, responsive, happy, and obedient. It really was an amazing dog in every way. I mentioned what I had noticed about the dog and the person I was standing with pointed up. I looked up and was shocked by what I saw. A large, black, mangy-looking dog was tied by a harness to a clothesline. The animal was muzzled, wrapped up, and tied from head to tail to paws in every way conceivable so that he could barely move. I wondered if the dog was still alive and was surprised to see his head and eyes move slightly as he watched us. My companion explained that the black dog had been an absolute disaster—relieving himself everywhere, never listening, and always destroying things. He explained that he had finally had enough and had fixed the problem.

As I woke up the whole thing seemed quite cruel, until God showed me what the dream meant.

To be continued...

FORGIVENESS

The shortest sermon I ever heard was on sin. The preacher said, "Don't!" and ended. I agree with the idea, but a little more information may be needed. I want to go a little beyond "Don't!" before talking about righteousness, so that no one's transformation is hindered by sin. Let's start by looking at one of my favorite Psalms, Psalm 51. In this Psalm David was given a prophetic revelation of the forgiveness, cleansing, and grace that was to come through Jesus.

The full story behind the Psalm is found in 2 Samuel 11, but here it is in brief: King David had stayed home when his army went out to battle. While he was walking on the roof of his palace he saw a beautiful woman below taking a bath. David found out that she was Bathsheba, the wife of Uriah, one of his soldiers. Uriah was away fighting for the Lord and for David. The king sent for her and slept with her. A short while later David received a message from Bathsheba informing him that she was pregnant. To try and cover up his sin, David immediately gave orders that Uriah was to bring him a report about the battle.

David kept Uriah home for three days in hopes that he would sleep with his wife. Unfortunately for David, Uriah wouldn't enter his own home or sleep with his wife. His sense of duty wouldn't allow him to relax while his fellow soldiers were still in battle. You'd think that perhaps the irony of the situation would have brought David to his senses—but no.

So David gave Uriah sealed orders to take back to his commander. In the letter he wrote: "*Put Uriah at the front of the fiercest fighting, then withdraw from him so that he is struck down and dies*" (2 Samuel 11:15). Uriah faithfully delivered those sealed orders. The report came back shortly that not only had Uriah been killed but several other soldiers were also killed carrying out David's orders. David seemed to take the news in stride. He basically said, "Well, people die in wars."

David had knowingly committed adultery, abused his authority, betrayed the trust of his soldiers, and committed mass murder to try and cover it all up. He had also betrayed God's trust, broken God's laws, and misused God's authority. And he had abused, taken advantage of, and murdered God's people (Psalm 51:4).

God told the prophet Nathan what David had done and sent him to confront David and deliver some very strict punishments. Fortunately for David, when he was confronted with his sin, he came to his senses. He finally realized the evil he had done and the pain he had caused, and he began to seriously repent (2 Samuel 12:13; Psalm 51:3–4). That's when he wrote Psalm 51.

> Be gracious to me, God, according to Your faithful love; according to Your abundant compassion, blot out my rebellion (Psalm 51:1).

David knew he deserved nothing but he also knew that God's love and mercy was huge, so he asked for a clean slate and for his sin to be completely blotted out. But he didn't stop there—he asked for more.

> Wash away my guilt and cleanse me from my sin. For I am conscious of my rebellion, and my sin is always before me (Psalm 51:2–3).

David was feeling guilt and shame and he couldn't shake it; so he boldly asked God to take that all away as well. But he didn't even stop there.

> Surely You desire integrity in the inner self, and You teach me wisdom deep within. Purify me with hyssop, and I will be clean; wash me, and I will be whiter than snow (Psalm 51:6–7).

David realized that something inside of him needed to be changed so that he wouldn't sin like this again. So he pushed further into mercy and asked God to teach him, cleanse him, and change him on the inside so he'd never repeat these things. But David still wasn't done.

> Let me hear joy and gladness; let the bones that You have crushed rejoice. Turn Your face away from my sins, and blot out all my guilt. God, create a clean heart for me, O God, and renew a steadfast spirit within me (Psalm 51:8–10).

David was feeling conscience-stricken about all of the pain he had caused. It's safe to say that he was a mental and emotional mess, deprived of all joy. David wanted to enjoy his relationship with God again, so he asked for a clean slate. But David still wasn't finished pressing in.

> Do not banish me from Your presence or take Your Holy Spirit from me. Restore the joy of Your salvation to me, and give me a willing spirit (Psalm 51:11–12).

As King of Israel, a soldier in God's army, a worshipper, and a prophet, David enjoyed God's intimate and very real presence (Psalm 16:11), and the power of God's Spirit anointing him to do all that he did. He desperately wanted to stay close to God. So he asked Him for yet more mercy. When David finished asking for mercy, forgiveness, and complete restoration, God helped him see something that we all need to understand.

> Then I will teach the rebellious Your ways, and sinners will return to You. Save me from the guilt of bloodshed, God, the God of my salvation, and my tongue will sing of Your righteousness. Lord, open my lips, and my mouth will declare Your praise (Psalm 51:13–15).

David knew that when he was restored he would give God all of the praise, and others would be encouraged to repent and receive the same amazing mercy.

The Spirit of God was prophetically revealing the kind of mercy, forgiveness, and complete restoration that is yours through the shed blood of Jesus. When you go to God He forgives you and wipes your record clean. Then He sets you free from guilt and shame and cleanses, teaches, and changes you on the inside, washing you whiter than snow so that you can walk free from sin. Then He sets you back on your feet and helps you enjoy Him and your life again. He continues to be close to you and use you for His glory. He restores your joy and because He's so amazing your lips are filled with His praises as you tell others of His awesome love.

John understood this and wrote:

> If we confess our sins, He is faithful and righteous to forgive us our sins <u>and to cleanse us from all unrighteousness</u> (1 John 1:9).

This one little verse sums up everything David prayed in Psalm 51. You must know that sin is unacceptable and confess it to God. When you do, He is faithful to forgive your sin and give you the entire cleansing *"from all unrighteousness"* that David prayed for. God has already poured out His mercy in Christ Jesus and He delights in forgiving, cleansing, and restoring you. It's a gift. In fact, when you walk with Jesus, sensitive to His Spirit in you, responding to Him, you continually walk under His mighty waterfall of transforming mercy and cleansing.

> If we walk in the light, as He is in the light, we have fellowship with one another, and the blood of Jesus His Son cleanses us from all sin (1 John 1:7).

The day that you believed in and accepted Jesus, you received God's mercy and all of your sins were forgiven. What you may not have known though is that all of these other things that David asked for are yours in Christ as well. If you feel like you've not been able to leave your sin completely behind you and walk with God in joy, then stop and pray this prayer (adapted from David's) from your heart:

> "Dear Holy Father, have mercy on me because of what Jesus accomplished on the cross. Please forgive me for all of my sins and wipe my record clean. Set me completely free from guilt and shame. Cleanse me and teach me, changing me on the inside, washing me whiter than snow so that I can walk free from every sin that has tripped me up. Set me back on my feet and help me to enjoy You and the life You've given me again, just as if the sin had never happened. I thank You that You have forgiven me and cleansed me, and that You continue to love me, be with me, and use me for Your purpose and glory. Please restore the joy of my salvation and continue to transform me into Christ's image. And let my lips be filled with praise, as I tell others of Your awesome mercy and love and Your cleansing, transforming power. I ask You and thank You for everything in Jesus' name. Amen."

RELATIONSHIP FIRST

Even though Jesus died once for all of your sins—past, present and future—it's important to go to the Father and talk to Him when you blow it (1 John 1:9). Jesus didn't die just so your sins could be forgiven but so that your relationship with Him (and with the Father and Holy Spirit) could be restored. You go to Him—your Father, Teacher and Counselor—with your sins and mistakes so you can get fathered, taught, and counseled.

You don't go to God because He's mad and won't forgive you unless you ask, but because you're in relationship with Him. Look at it like a marriage. What if a husband was miserable to his wife one day and then acted like it never happened the next? Could the husband say, "Well, you already vowed to love me for better or worse and yesterday was a 'worse' day." That wouldn't go over very well. Although the husband should be able to rely on his wife's commitment to love him always, to take it for granted would show that he had lost sight that their marriage is much more than a set of vows.

Between your conscience and the Holy Spirit inside of you you'll know when it's time to talk with your Father about any wrong behavior. You can always trust that you are forgiven and cleansed of the sins that you don't even know you're committing (Psalm 19:12–14; 1 John 1:7–9). Also, you don't need to talk to God again about sins you've already addressed, since He's very good at forgiving and forgetting.

God wants you looking forward to His goal for you, the image of Jesus, never back. By His grace, leave the past behind (2 Corinthians 7:10; Romans 8:1; Philippians 3:12–14; Lamentations 3:22–24).

Now let's look at how God's gift of righteousness sets you up for transformation.

THE GIFT OF RIGHTEOUSNESS

You may tend to think that someone is good if they're mostly good and/or better than others, but righteousness, from God's standpoint, is not like that. Righteousness is *being* right and perfect and *doing* what is right and perfect—according to God's standard—in your relationship with God and with people. God's standard for righteousness is set by Him alone.

You are either accepted by God as righteous or you are not. There is no grey area.

Righteousness in the Bible has a "declared" aspect and an "actual" one. God can both declare someone righteous—like a court could declare someone innocent—and cause someone to actually *be* righteous. Before Jesus came only a few people (such as Abraham and Job) had been declared righteous and not one person had ever actually been totally righteousness (Romans 3:10). The good news is that through faith in Jesus you are declared righteous by God.

> But now, apart from the law, God's righteousness has been revealed... that is, God's righteousness through faith in Jesus Christ, to all who believe, since there is no distinction (Romans 3:21–22).

> He made the One who did not know sin to be sin for us, so that we might become the righteousness of God in Him (2 Corinthians 5:21).

What these verses are talking about is an amazing truth that is often called the "Great Exchange." Jesus took your sin and you were given His righteousness. Your sin and your old self are forgotten and God declares you to be His redeemed, righteous, newly-created children. It's important that you understand that when you're forgiven you're not just *barely* out of the doghouse or the penalty box; God has declared you righteous and sees you as righteous. Paul called it "the gift of righteousness" (Romans 5:17). That's amazing, but there's more included in the gift.

> You took off your former way of life, the old self that is corrupted by deceitful desires; you are being renewed in the spirit of your minds; <u>you put on the new self, the one created according to God's likeness in righteousness</u> and purity of the truth (Ephesians 4:22–24).

In these verses Paul shows that you're not just *declared* righteous because of what Jesus did, you actually become righteous. You are to "put on" or become the new creation, which has already been *"created according to God's likeness in righteousness."* Remember, you are saved, being saved, and you will be saved. The same is true of righteousness—when you were saved you were declared righteous, you are now being made righteous, and when you see Him, you will be as He is, righteous.

Years ago I thought that having the "gift of righteousness" meant that God would always consider me righteous and that I just needed to do my best to behave. I was very glad to discover that I was wrong. God declares you righteous and then Jesus and the Holy Spirit make you righteous; it's one gift, the gift of righteousness. Obviously, you cannot be transformed and become more like Jesus, the Righteous One, without actually growing in righteousness.

> For just as through one man's disobedience the many were made sinners, so also through the one man's obedience <u>the many will be made righteous</u> (Romans 5:19).

Because of Adam's sin we were all made sinners and because of this, we sinned. Now through faith in Jesus we are made righteous and because of this, we become righteous.

Jesus is your mediator and guarantor. He has done everything needed to declare you righteous and to make you righteous, just like Him. He has undertaken to walk with you, teach you, work within you, and transform you into His righteous image! God said, "Let there be light" and it came into being. God said, "You are my righteousness" and you became/become His righteousness. The gift of righteousness is meant to be unwrapped.

My previous understanding of the "gift of righteousness" fell far short of God's goal. In a sense I was believing that God was unable to make me righteous so He looked at Jesus instead of me and pretended that I was righteous. No! Paul said, "*He gave Himself for us to redeem us from all lawlessness and to cleanse for Himself a people for His own possession, eager to do good works*" (Titus 2:14).

In Psalm 51 you read about David discovering God's mercy to completely forgive, cleanse, and restore him from his sins. In Christ Jesus God has declared you righteous and has undertaken to cleanse you from *all* unrighteousness (1 John 1:9) in every area of your life and make you righteous like Him. What David prayed for has now become your expectation for restoration.

The Bible is full of verses about how the righteous are blessed by God. To be declared righteous and to be made righteous is to live the life God meant for you.

THE FATHER OF OUR FAITH

Our understanding of the "gift of righteousness" is often taken from what Paul wrote in Romans chapter four about Abraham.

> If Abraham was justified by works, he has something to brag about—but not before God. For what does the Scripture say? Abraham believed God, and it was credited to him for righteousness. Now to the one who works, pay is not considered as a gift, but as something owed. But to the one who does not work, but believes on Him <u>who declares the ungodly to be righteous</u>, his faith is credited for righteousness (Romans 4:2–5).

Paul was quoting from Genesis 15:6. In that chapter God showed Abraham the night sky and told him his descendants would be as numerous as the stars. Abraham believed God and God declared Him righteous. That event is a picture of the moment you believed in Jesus, were saved and declared righteous; but the picture doesn't stop there. Abraham's faith and God's declaration changed Abraham and led him into a life of obeying and following God (Hebrews 11:8–10). Paul's point wasn't, "All you need is faith"; his point was that faith, not works, leads to righteousness—declared and actual.

Let's look at what James said about Abraham's life and righteousness:

> Wasn't Abraham our father justified by works when he offered Isaac his son on the altar? <u>You see that faith was active together with his works, and by works, faith was perfected. So the Scripture was fulfilled</u> that says, Abraham believed God, and it was credited to him for righteousness, and he was called God's friend. You see that a man is justified by works and not by faith alone (James 2:21–24).

James is saying that Abraham was declared righteous and the fulfillment of that declaration was demonstrated by Abraham's righteous actions.

Paul called Abraham the father of all who believe (Romans 4:16). His life pictured the gift of righteousness that is now yours—the children of the promise through Christ Jesus (Romans 4:23–25, Galatians 3:16, 23). He's your example and you live as he did, in a righteousness—declared and actual—that comes by faith. God gave you the gift of righteousness so that you could open it and enjoy being transformed into all He created you to be.

ROOM TO GROW

The Bible talks about believers being like newborn spiritual children who are to grow up into maturity (Matthew 18:3; 1 Corinthians 3:2; Hebrews 5:12; 1 Peter 2:2). An earthly dad doesn't expect a toddler to know what an adult knows; he gives his child room to grow up. Just so—because of your declared righteousness—God sees you as a new creation in Christ (2 Corinthians 5:17; Ephesians 4:24) and gives you the room you need to grow.

It's important that you understand that God didn't declare you righteousness so that He could pretend you're righteous or to give you permission to continue in sin. God is your Dad. He sent His Son to bring you home so that you could know Him and be transformed. He doesn't want to miss a moment of your growth. He wants to walk with you and work in you and know great satisfaction when He sees you trust Him, follow Jesus, and become more like Him.

Now let's talk about God's grace.

GRACE

Grace has been defined as "God's unmerited favor" and is often summed up by the acronym, "God's Riches At Christ's Expense." However, when it comes to the "being saved" part of your salvation, it's not the precise definition that's important; what matters is grace's practical purpose. What you need to understand is, grace is what tethers you to everything you need for living and growing in Christ in every circumstance and in every moment.

God decided to make you in His image and likeness before you were even born. He decided to take all of the responsibility for accomplishing that on Himself and give it to you as a gift. You are forgiven, cleansed, redeemed, saved, made righteous, made new, adopted into God's family, restored, given new and eternal life, indwelt by His Spirit, loved, blessed, cared for, directed, taught, and transformed—all as a gift because of what Jesus did. That's God's grace.

Sin worked in you when you were spiritually dead and made you sin. You didn't have to work at being sinners, it was a free result of your first birth as descendants of Adam. Sin reigned in you. Now that you've been born in Christ and declared righteousness, sin has lost its power and God's grace reigns. God's grace reigns in you, obliterating the reign of sin and supplying everything you need to be transformed into His image (Romans 5:19–21). Your salvation and sanctification come with "batteries included" and those powerful batteries are charged by God's grace (2 Timothy 2:1).

If grace had a name it would be "Jesus" because everything you need for your salvation—past, present and future—was supplied as a gift because of what He did for you.

I believe the Apostle Paul summed up the effect of God's grace in this one verse:

> But by God's grace <u>I am what I am</u>, and His grace toward me was not ineffective. However, I worked more than any of them, <u>yet not I, but God's grace that was with me</u> (1 Corinthians 15:10).

All who Paul had become and everything he accomplished was all because of God's grace. God's Word encourages you to follow Jesus the way Paul did.

GRACE: THE KINGDOM'S ROAD

The road that leads to you getting saved and being saved is called "Grace." You get into the Kingdom by God's grace and you walk in it by grace. This metaphorical road has a ditch on each side. The two ditches are called "Works" and "Grace Misunderstood." Paul talked about both ditches in relation to grace.

The "Grace Misunderstood" Ditch

> What should we say then? <u>Should we continue in sin in order that grace may multiply? Absolutely not! How can we who died to sin still live in it?</u> ... just as Christ was raised from the dead by the glory of the Father, <u>so we too may walk in a new way of life</u> (Romans 6:1–2, 4).

Paul was clear that seeing grace as an excuse to stay in sin was completely missing the point. *"How can we who died to sin still live in it?"* As baptism pictures, your old self is dead and buried in Christ Jesus and you are raised with Him to a *"new way of life."*

But you're not under law, right? Paul spent much time teaching that Christians are no longer under the Jewish law. He did so because his audience included Jewish people and it needed to be clarified. Modern Christians—being very distant culturally from that original setting—tend to read those verses to mean that there are no behavioral standards for Christians. Paul never meant nor said that. His point was that following a set of external laws and relying on your ability to keep those laws will not make you right with God. Paul never taught that you were free to do as you please and that God would forgive you anyway. You were *declared* righteous so you could *become* righteous.

"Works" Ditch

> Did you receive the Spirit by the works of the law or by hearing with faith? Are you so foolish? <u>After beginning with the Spirit, are you now going to be made complete by the flesh</u>? (Galatians 3:1–3).

Paul also stated that thinking that once you're saved, you can please God in your own efforts or do the "being saved" part on your own is foolish. *"After beginning with the Spirit, are you now going to be made complete by the flesh?"* Why try to earn righteousness or be righteous in your own strength when you've already been given the gift of His righteousness and He's promised to work it in you?

Paul taught that you have been set free from both sin and your own self-reliant effort. That's both ditches. Grace without growth is license to sin. Change without grace is works. Transformation by His grace is the New Covenant.

Jesus' work was complete; by God's grace you come into the Kingdom and by that same powerful grace you are being saved, made righteous, and being transformed into Christ's image.

> <u>We too all previously lived among them in our fleshly desires, carrying out the inclinations of our flesh and thoughts</u>, and by nature we were children under wrath, as the others were also.... <u>For you are saved by grace through faith</u>, and this is not from yourself; it is God's gift — not from works, so that no one can boast. <u>For we are His creation, created in Christ Jesus for good works, which God prepared ahead of time so that we should walk in them</u> (Ephesians 2:3, 7–10).

Grace is meant to take you from being lost and in sin (verse 3) to being His creation, walking in Christ, and doing the good works He's prepared for you to do (verse 10). You cannot boast in your getting saved nor in your transformation because it's all *"by grace through faith."* To walk down the center of God's Grace Road and stay out of both ditches is to believe that He's declared you righteous and He's at work within you making you righteous. His grace brought you in, His grace grows you up, and by His grace you'll receive all He has for you in eternity.

My dream continued...

In my dream about two dogs, one was well behaved and running around free; the other was uncontrollable and disobedient and had been securely harnessed to a clothesline.

> Since you have heard about Jesus and have learned the truth that comes from him, <u>throw off your old sinful nature and your former way of life, which is corrupted by lust and deception</u>. Instead, let the Spirit renew your thoughts and attitudes. <u>Put on your new nature, created to be like God— truly righteousness and holy</u> (Ephesians 4:21–24 NLT).

Your old self is *"corrupted by lust and deception"* and your new self is *"created to be like God — truly righteousness and holy."* The old self is dead in Christ, but as in the dream, it seems like it's just bound and gagged. Transformation is a process and you can still choose to untie your old dog and let it run amuck. Instead you need to believe that you've been made righteous and that everything you need to become righteous is supplied by grace. Then you can put off the old self and put on the new self; and as you do you grow in His righteousness.

Spend some time talking to Him about what you have just read.

Next, look at another very important element of your transformation. If your salvation—past, present and future—is all by grace through faith, you should not only have a clear understanding of grace, but also of faith.

POWER POINTS FROM TRUTH NUMBER 3
Quotes for Sharing on Social Media

The shortest sermon I ever heard was on sin. The preacher said, "Don't!" and ended.

∼

God has already poured out His mercy in Christ Jesus and He delights in forgiving, cleansing, and restoring you. It's a gift.

∼

You go to Him—your Father, Teacher and Counselor—with your sins and mistakes so you can get fathered, taught, and counseled.

∼

You don't need to talk to God again about sins you've already addressed, since He's very good at forgiving and forgetting.

∼

God wants you looking forward to His goal for you, the image of Jesus, never back. By His grace, leave the past behind.

*Your sin and your old self are forgotten and God declares you
to be His redeemed, righteous, newly-created children.*

∽

*God declares you righteous and then Jesus and the Holy Spirit
make you righteous; it's one gift, the gift of righteousness.*

∽

*You cannot be transformed and become more like Jesus,
the Righteous One, without actually growing in righteousness.*

∽

*Paul's point wasn't, "All you need is faith"; his point was that
faith, not works, leads to righteousness—declared and actual.*

∽

*Abraham was declared righteous and the fulfillment of that declaration
was demonstrated by Abraham's righteous actions.*

∽

*Grace is what tethers you to everything you need for living and
growing in Christ in every circumstance and in every moment.*

∽

*God's grace reigns in you, obliterating the reign of sin and
supplying everything you need to be transformed into His image.*

∽

*Salvation and sanctification come with "batteries included"
and those powerful batteries are charged by God's grace.*

∽

If grace had a name it would be "Jesus."

*Grace without growth is license to sin.
Change without grace is works.
Transformation by His grace is the New Covenant.*

∼

His grace brought you in, His grace grows you up, and by His grace you'll receive all He has for you in eternity.

From Faith to Faith

Truth Number 4

Everything you need to be transformed from within has been supplied but it won't happen by itself; you need to receive it and walk in it by faith.

My Dream

I was preparing for a trip and packing. I turned away to grab something else that I needed to pack. When I turned back I saw the torso of myself (head and body with no arms or legs) lying down in my suitcase. It (my torso) was working against me, doing its best to squirm and mess up my shirts and cause what I'd packed to fall out of the suitcase. I began trying to pack and repack with more determination and effort and my torso responded in kind. The harder I tried the harder it worked at defeating my efforts. As the battle came to a crescendo I started yelling for help, the calls for help quickly grew louder and more violent as I fought more desperately. I woke up quite disturbed; "torso man" had a horror about him and he was fierce in his determination.

God gave me this dream before He started teaching me about being transformed into Christ's image by grace through faith. The dream and my response to it showed that after a couple of decades of being a Christian I may have understood the definitions of the words, grace, righteousness, and faith, but I didn't fully understand how they were all meant to work together to transform me.

To be continued...

We've talked about righteousness and grace, now let's look at faith and then look at how they all work together.

"FAITH" AND "THE FAITH"

Please read these verses thoughtfully:

> <u>Now without faith it is impossible to please God</u>, for the one who draws near to Him must believe that He exists and rewards those who seek Him (Hebrews 11:6).

> <u>But let him ask in faith</u> without doubting. For the doubter is like the surging sea, driven and tossed by the wind. <u>That person should not expect to receive anything from the Lord</u> (James 1:6–7).

Since it's impossible to please God or have your prayers answered without faith, understanding faith should be a priority. However, there is much fog surrounding the topic of faith; but there need not be because the Bible teaches about faith in a really straightforward way. First let's clear up the sometimes confusing difference between "faith" and "the Faith." According to the dictionary, the word "faith" has two different basic categories of meaning. One has to do with the trust or confidence you put in someone or something—often without proof. The second carries the meaning of a system of religious belief. So you could say, "I belong to the Christian Faith" and you can tell God, "I have faith in You," and be talking about two completely different definitions of the word.

I could be part of the Christian Faith and believe in God and yet constantly doubt God. The Disciples were definitely part of the Faith yet Jesus reproved them many times for their "*lack of faith.*" The generation of Israelites who spent 40 years in the wilderness believed in God, but they died in the wilderness because they didn't have faith that God would help them conquer the Promised Land (Hebrews 4:19).

So "the Faith" is about a general faith in God, Jesus, the truth of the Bible, the tenets of Christianity, etc. It's a passive faith or something you just simply believe to be true. Having faith that God will do what He said He will do is specific, topical, and requires your active involvement. James says that if you want wisdom from God, you must ask in faith, without doubting that He is going to give it to you. So a person can be strong in "the Faith" and still not receive wisdom from God because they don't have faith that God will give it to them. In this section we'll be talking about that specific and active faith and how you use it to walk in your transformation.

ACTIVE FAITH

The best place to start investigating active faith is by looking at the Bible verse that defines it.

> Now faith is the reality of things hoped for, the proof of what is not seen (Hebrews 11:1).

Let's look at one of the words in faith's definition. In today's culture when you talk about something you "hope" for you are generally talking about something that you wish would happen, something that may or may not happen. However, Biblical hope looks forward to things that are certain and true but are still unseen. For example, you hope for your new glorified body that the Bible says you'll receive when Jesus comes back.

> ...we also groan within ourselves, eagerly waiting for adoption, the redemption of our bodies. <u>Now in this hope, we were saved, yet hope that is seen is not hope, because who hopes for what he sees</u>? (Romans 8:23–24).

So if faith is the substance of things hoped for—guaranteed but not yet seen—then faith is your inward response to what God says is true, or your choice to believe it. Faith is a decision to believe that changes a worldly "I hope so" to the biblical "I know so." Here's a simple illustration: if you walked up to a group of young kids at your church and told them that there were ice cream cones for all of them in the kitchen, their reaction would demonstrate hope and faith. If they instantly believed you, then they've made that ice cream their hope and they have faith. When they start running towards the kitchen, they're acting in faith. You use faith to make God's promises your hope and see them come to pass in your life.

Let's expand on the ice cream example; if every time you've done this there was ice cream in the kitchen, then the kids believe you because they trust you. They make your announcement their hope and run in faith to the kitchen. You don't trust God because He demands it; you trust God because He's trustworthy (Psalm 9:10). So when you find out what God has promised to do, because you trust Him you can make that your hope.

> For indeed the gospel was preached to us as well as to them; but the word which they heard did not profit them, not being mixed with faith in those who heard it (Hebrews 4:2 NKJV).

When the Israelites first got to the border of the Promised Land Moses sent twelve spies into the land to scout it out. Ten came back full of fear. Two, Joshua and Caleb, returned saying, "If God has given us this land then He'll help us take it." However, the ten convinced the people of the impossibility of the task and consequently they all spent forty needless years in the wilderness—and died there. The people didn't mix faith with what God said. Instead of believing God and making the Promised Land their hope, they looked at the difficulties and doubted, and therefore didn't receive what God had promised. Remember, the Israelites had just seen God rescue them from Egypt, part the Red Sea, and drown the Egyptian army. Believing *in* God wasn't the problem; the problem was they didn't believe that God would do this specific thing He had promised to do.

Abraham got it right. God promised him that he would have a son. Even though he and Sarah were too old to have kids, Abraham believed it and that promise became his hope.

> He believed, hoping against hope, so that he became the father of many nations according to what had been spoken: So will your descendants be.... <u>He did not waver in unbelief at God's promise</u> but was strengthened in his faith and gave glory to God, <u>because he was fully convinced that what He had promised He was also able to perform</u>. Therefore it was credited to him for righteousness (Romans 4:18, 20–22).

These verses are a great picture of the mechanics of faith. God promised something specific to Abraham that Abraham desired but couldn't dare to hope for because it was impossible. But when God promised it, Abraham believed. Why was Abraham able to not waver in unbelief? He stopped looking at what was normal and plausible and kept his eyes on Him who is faithful and able.

Faith is not always easy but it holds on to God's promise despite circumstances because God is able to change circumstances. So back to the ice cream: what happens if the kids find the kitchen closed and locked? Some kids will shrug or groan and go find their parents. But the kids who stick by their faith in you and their hope for ice cream, will realize that you wouldn't lead them astray and they'll refuse to give up. They'll knock on the kitchen door or run back to you and get your help. Those kids will end up with their hope realized.

If you walk in faith like Abraham did you will please God and have your prayers answered. To do that you must find out what God's will is through His Word and prayer. Then you choose to trust Him, and use your faith to turn your "wishful thinking" into biblical hope. Finally, you need to turn your eyes away from your circumstances and keep them fixed on your faithful, loving, and miraculous God—even when your faith is tested.

GOD'S NAVIGATIONAL TOOL

Getting saved by grace through faith was quite easy; you heard the Gospel, put your hope in the message and your faith in God and responded. You didn't even know what trust, hope, and faith meant, yet you were swept along. The final realization of your salvation is quite simple as well. It'll happen in an instant when the time comes. However, the big middle part of "being saved" or being transformed into the image of Jesus requires that you live by faith daily.

Think of Abraham again, the father of your faith. God pronounced Him righteous in a second and when he died, he was *"gathered to his people"* (Genesis 25:7) in a second. However, he needed to trust God and walk by faith for his whole life in between those two seconds. Likewise, "being saved" must be received by faith and that's why understanding faith is so important. But why is faith necessary? (See James 1:6–7.) The answer is quite simple.

The first part of the answer is found in the biblical definition of faith and is well illustrated by the Israelites coming out of bondage in Egypt. Hebrews 11:1 says, *"Now faith is the reality of what is hoped for, the proof of what is not seen."* Much of what God calls you to believe is *"not seen"* when you're first asked to believe; therefore you need faith to believe it. With some things, like the reality of heaven, you just need to believe and there is no action required on your part. However, in regards to many other "unseen" issues, faith is a practical navigational tool and is needed to facilitate your obedience.

God told the Israelites that He was going to deliver them from Egypt and give them the Promised Land. Their faith wasn't really involved in their deliverance from Egypt. They mostly watched as the plagues came and went and the Red Sea parted. However, taking the Promised Land wasn't going to happen overnight; it required their ongoing obedience. Faith was now required as a navigational tool. They needed it to help them keep heading in God's direction. It was time for the Israelites to demonstrate their faith by obeying God even though they couldn't see the outcome yet. Unfortunately they didn't.

You need faith to believe that you are a new creation and that you're being transformed into the image of Jesus—but it won't happen overnight and it won't often "feel" like it's happening. Faith is essential because God calls you to an unseen destination and asks you to head in that direction; faith is one of God's key navigational tools.

> <u>By faith</u> Abraham, when he was called, obeyed and went out to a place he was going to receive as an inheritance. <u>He went out not knowing where he was going</u> (Hebrews 11:8).

FAITH AND GRACE

The second reason why faith is necessary is also wonderfully profound. Remember, *nothing* in the New Covenant is received because of your works. You cannot earn any of it. It's all by grace. If you could earn even the smallest part of anything Jesus did for you, then you could boast. But the Bible is clear that you cannot.

> But it is <u>from Him</u> that you are in Christ Jesus, who became God-given wisdom for us—our righteousness, sanctification, and redemption, in order that, as it is written: <u>The one who boasts must boast in the Lord</u> (1 Corinthians 1:30–31).

Your salvation, your wisdom, your righteousness, your redemption, and your sanctification—which is God's process for transforming you into Christ's image—are all provided for in Christ. Once you understand that *everything* in your getting saved, being saved, and realizing your final salvation is all by grace then you can understand the absolute necessity of faith. Read this verse carefully.

> <u>This is why the promise is by faith, so that it may be according to grace, to guarantee it to all the descendants</u>—not only to those who are of the law but also to those who are of Abraham's faith (Romans 4:16).

If a single part of your salvation depended on your works God could not "*guarantee*" it because you could fail. So in His great love for you God gave you everything as a free gift—grace—so that nothing would depend on your works and God could guarantee the outcome. If everything is a free gift then the only way you can receive it is by faith in the gift-giver.

Let's go back to the ice cream example. Picture this: You announce, "Ice cream for everyone!" Some kids hoot and holler and run to the kitchen, but others put their heads down and shuffle slowly off. You intercept the kids doing the Eeyore impersonation and ask why they're not heading to the kitchen. Two of the kids explain that they have no money; the other tells you sadly that he doesn't deserve a treat because he didn't do well with his memory verse. What's your response?

You're giving the ice cream as a gift so everyone qualifies and is guaranteed a treat, therefore the kids cannot earn it. They must receive your grace. That's what Paul said in Romans 4:16 that everything God has for you is given freely by grace. God arranged it that way so that His promises could be guaranteed. And because it's all a gift, the only way you can get it is by faith, by believing that God has freely given it to you. If you could receive anything from God in any other way than through faith it wouldn't be by grace.

That's why it's impossible to please God without faith (Hebrews 11:6), because without it, you cannot receive His grace.

> Now if by grace, then it is not by works; otherwise grace ceases to be grace (Romans 11:6).

The minute you start thinking that you deserve anything from God, that you can please Him yourself, or that you can become more like Christ yourself, grace ceases to be grace in your life.

HOPE DESIRED EQUALS FAITH INSPIRED

Abraham didn't worry about how impossible his hope was or about whether he deserved it or not. Instead, he kept His eyes on Him who is faithful and able, and held fast to the hope of having a son (Romans 4:18–22). That's an example of how you receive God's promise to form His Son in you (Galatians 4:19).

> And we all, with unveiled face, <u>beholding the glory of the Lord</u>, are being transformed into the same image from one degree of glory to another (2 Corinthians 3:18 ESV).

Abraham kept his eyes on God and his hope set on having a son. In the same way, you keep your eyes on Jesus your Master and Teacher and your hope set on being transformed into His image. You are transformed by walking down the center of the road called Grace—by faith—with your eyes on Him and your unseen hope.

An important constant in these examples is that hope is set on something you desire; kids love ice cream, Abraham really wanted a son, and Joshua and Caleb wanted to get into that amazing Promised Land. What God has in store for you in your transformation is so jaw-dropping it's beyond your imagining. (See Ephesians 3:20.)

Faith inspired by its desired hope doesn't sit still—it gets up and heads towards it. The Israelites who died in the wilderness demonstrated their unbelief by refusing to enter the Promised Land. A generation later, the ones who believed God demonstrated their hope and faith by crossing the Jordan River. Mental assent to a truth is not faith. Saying, "I believe that," and then going back to life as usual is not faith. Faith grabs hold of your hope and gets you up and moving towards it, and when obstacles block the way, it keeps you moving. If the promise of transformation into His image—becoming all God created and predestined you to be—has now become your hope, grab hold by faith and don't let go.

Take a minute to ask the Father to help you see the potential of being transformed into His image and walking in all that He has for you. Ask Him to make it your desired hope so it inspires your faith.

FAITH IS A GIFT

Here are two last questions before you move on: If faith is a prerequisite to receiving His grace, then isn't faith a kind of works? And how can your transformation be guaranteed if faith is required; what if you don't have that kind of faith? I've wrestled with these same questions.

First, as you've seen with the ice cream illustration, faith is quite simple. Faith isn't a magic substance, it's a choice to believe God that is made and powered by His grace. Sometimes you overcomplicate faith and then struggle with a lack of faith in your own faith and other such mental gymnastics. Abraham decided that God could and would do what He said He'd do—then he stuck with that decision no matter what. That's faith.

Jesus had great faith and He is transforming you into His image. So as you grow in Him, your faith will grow beyond what you can currently imagine, as He works in you. Since I realized that, my faith seems to increase weekly. He's the one taking me there and increasing my faith from *"glory to glory."*

Jesus works faith in you; He establishes your hope, helps you choose to believe and helps you deal with unbelief all by His grace. Hebrews 12:2 calls Jesus *"the source and perfecter of our faith."* His complete work on your behalf needed to include help with your faith (2 Peter 1:3); simply because without it, you can't receive His grace. He's at work within you causing you to want to believe and causing you to believe.

I should explain here that doubts and unbelief are two different things. Doubts are just pesky thoughts that challenge your faith. Unbelief is choosing not to believe what God has said. When the Israelites decided to believe the ten fearful spies (Numbers 13–14) instead of God, they chose unbelief instead of faith. Not good. When you decide to believe God you put unbelief behind you, but thoughts will still flit through your head that challenge your faith decision. Those are doubts. Doubts are a normal part of the process and show that you're currently working with the Lord to change the way you think.

James talked about the "doubter" (James 1:6–8). He was referring to the one who hasn't decided to believe or not believe. Just because you experience doubts doesn't mean you're a "doubter." Once you've decided to trust God for something that He's promised, the doubts may come; but every time one passes through your mind, shoot it down by reiterating what you've chosen to believe.

My wife and I prayed for someone and God instantly did a miracle in her body. Even though she knew God had healed her she continued to give voice to her doubt, wondering if she'd stay healed, etc. So I asked her, "What do golfers do?" She replied, "Golf." I asked her, "What do swimmers do?" She replied, "Swim." Then I asked, "What do Believers do?" She hesitated and as she answered slowly, I could tell she had made the right choice.

So here's what you need to choose to believe and pray:

"Thank You, Father, that You have declared me righteous; my past is gone, my sins are forgiven and forgotten. You've cleansed me and given me all things new. I am Your child. You, by Your great expression of love called grace, are causing me to be righteous and awesome. Your Holy Spirit is working within me causing me to *want* to do and to *do* Your will. Father, I thank You that You are always with me, loving me, teaching me, and transforming me into Your image, making me into all You created and called me to be."

Before we stop talking about faith I would like to talk to you about one of the most encouraging things God ever showed me about being transformed.

JESUS DID IT FIRST

Every time my good friend and brother-in-law hears someone use a big word he says, "Never use a big word when a diminutive one will do." Unfortunately, a diminutive one will not do here. The term "hypostatic union" is a technical term that describes the fact that Jesus was—and is—fully human and fully divine—fully man and fully God.

Although Jesus is God, knows everything, is all-powerful and omnipresent, He temporarily put that aside to become human (Philippians 2:7). That's not saying that He ceased being God—He is "Immanuel" which means "God with us" (Isaiah 7:14)—but in order to be able to identify fully with you He chose to become like you in every way.

> For we do not have a high priest who is unable to sympathize with our weaknesses, but one who in every respect has been tempted as we are, yet without sin (Hebrews 4:15; see also Philippians 2:6–8; Hebrews 2:14).

It would be a little difficult for you to hear Jesus say, "I understand, I also went through that" if you knew that He had used His "get out of anything free" God-card whenever things got tough. In order to be your high priest Jesus needed to keep His God-card put away and live His life here as an example to us. So when Jesus came here as a baby, He *"emptied Himself"* of all His divine power (Philippians 2:7) and put Himself entirely in the hands of the Father. When He was born, even though He was God, He had to learn and grow just like a regular child—He didn't come out of Mary's womb talking and teaching. The scripture describes Him growing and learning as a kid in the usual way.

> And Jesus increased in wisdom and stature, and in favor with God and with people (Luke 2:52).

One of the interesting discussions that has come out of this truth is: at what point did Jesus fully realize who He was and how did that happen? Luke chapter two shows you that Jesus had a good idea by the age of twelve (Luke 2:49). However, I think the "why" is more important than the "when," and the "why" is amazing! As your example, Jesus went through what you go through in discovering who God says you are and what He's called you to do (Hebrews 4:15).

Once you are born of God you need to learn who God created you to be and what He created you to do and then progressively be transformed into His image and accomplish His plan for you, all by faith. Jesus progressively learned who He was, why He was here and what He needed to accomplish—all under the grace and care of His heavenly Father, by faith.

Jesus learned who He was and what He was to do all through God's Word and the Holy Spirit within Him, just like you are to do. Jesus had to learn that He was not only the Messiah but that He was God—and He had to not doubt that! Then He had to walk in that by faith. The Bible and the Holy Spirit tell you that you are forgiven, a very child of God, a new creation in Christ who is righteous in Him, created for good works, a temple of the Holy Spirit, who is being transformed into His image, and called to change the world. You are to follow Jesus' example, believe God's Word, embrace what it says about you and, by grace through faith, walk it out; you are to follow Him.

If you think it's hard for you to believe what God's Word says about you, think of Jesus: as a man, He had to learn and then choose to believe that He was the eternal Son of God who had created everything, who had come to die a brutal death at the hands of those He came to save. In light of that, your task seems quite a bit easier! The good news for you is that Jesus has already walked through it, understands the process, and is now with you to help you walk it out. The other big chunk of good news is that all of heaven's attention and resources were made available to ensure Jesus' success and all of the same attention and resources are available, in the same way, to ensure yours.

My dream continued…

The "torso Rick" dream came as I was just starting to learn to be transformed by grace through faith. So at first, I thought God was calling me to bring torso Rick under more strict control. God must have chuckled at me as He saw me double my efforts to straighten myself out. (Honestly, knowing what I know now, I don't even know how I got that message out of that dream.) So I made commitments to myself to do "more of this and less of that" and went through a series of systems and ideas to bring myself under control. Everything I tried lasted for a very short time and each time I eventually found myself back exactly where I started. Torso Rick kept winning round after round and I was getting more fearful that I would be unable to completely obey God. It was frustrating!

As God taught me more I began to realize that when you fear failure, you have your eyes on your abilities instead of His empowering grace, and you fail again and again. I asked God to help me put my faith in what Jesus did and what He promised to do in me. Then I locked my hope on God transforming me into Christ's image and my faith was set. Doubts floated through my head screaming at me, but I thanked God all the louder that He was in control and at work within me by His Spirit and grace.

Within a week of finally really getting it, giving these things to the Lord, and staying locked in by faith, my desires and behaviors started changing. More importantly, the fear of not pleasing God was replaced with the hope that God's grace was more than enough to transform me.

I did not abandon myself to torso Rick and say, "Oh well, God will change me if He wants to." That would have been climbing out of the "Works" ditch only to dive into the "Grace Misunderstood" ditch. I kept moving towards righteousness; I merely kept my focus on His work and strength instead of mine. And every time I slipped up, I got up, talked to God and kept trusting in His grace and standing in faith. Your faith keeps you believing God's promises, interacting with Him relationally and moving towards His perfect will.

In the dream God was showing me that I was fighting a losing battle and that I needed a new strategy—and I'm very grateful that His plan was to teach me that new strategy.

Whether you're struggling with sin or to change the way you think, speak, or behave—or you're looking to draw closer to Him or do what He's called you to do—whatever it is, ask God to transform you and make you like Jesus in that area. Then rest in His complete work, stand in His grace by faith, and watch Him change you from the inside-out as you move in obedience.

Take a few moments to talk to Him about the areas of your life that you've been struggling with. You've been forgiven and declared righteous; now trust Him to cleanse you and establish that righteousness in you by grace.

Next, I'd like to talk about how entirely complete what Jesus did for you was and is. There is nothing in yourself, in your life, in this world, or in hell that can hold you back from being transformed into the amazing new creation God made you to be.

POWER POINTS FROM TRUTH NUMBER 4
Quotes for Sharing on Social Media

Since it's impossible to please God or have your prayers answered without faith, understanding faith should be a priority.

∼

Having faith that God will do what He said He will do is specific, topical, and requires your active involvement.

∼

Biblical hope looks forward to things that are certain and true but are still unseen.

∼

Faith is a decision to believe that changes a worldly "I hope so" to the biblical "I know so."

∼

You use faith to make God's promises your hope and see them come to pass in your life.

∼

You don't trust God because He demands it; you trust God because He's trustworthy (Psalm 9:10).

∼

Faith is not always easy but it holds on to God's promise despite circumstances because God is able to change circumstances.

∼

Faith is essential because God calls you to an unseen destination and asks you to head in that direction.

God gave you everything as a free gift—grace—so that nothing would depend on your works and God could guarantee the outcome.

∼

If you could receive anything from God in any other way than through faith it wouldn't be by grace.

∼

It's impossible to please God without faith (Hebrews 11:6), because without it, you cannot receive His grace.

∼

You are transformed by walking down the center of the road called Grace—by faith—with your eyes on Him and your unseen hope.

∼

Faith grabs hold of your hope and gets you up and moving towards it, and when obstacles block the way, it keeps you moving.

∼

Faith isn't a magic substance, it's a choice to believe God that is made and powered by His grace.

∼

Abraham decided that God could and would do what He said He'd do—then he stuck with that decision no matter what. That's faith.

Jesus had great faith and He is transforming you into His image. So as you grow in Him, your faith will grow.

∼

Jesus works faith in you; He establishes your hope, helps you choose to believe and helps you deal with unbelief all by His grace.

*Doubts are just pesky thoughts that challenge your faith.
Unbelief is choosing not to believe what God has said.*

∽

*Father, I thank You that You are always with me, loving me,
teaching me, and transforming me into Your image.*

∽

*In order to be your high priest Jesus needed to keep His God-card
put away and live His life here as an example to us.*

∽

*As your example, Jesus went through what you go through in
discovering who God says you are and what He's called you to do.*

∽

*You are to follow Jesus' example, believe God's Word, embrace
what it says about you and, by grace through faith, walk it out.*

∽

*When you fear failure, you have your eyes on your abilities instead
of His empowering grace, and you fail again and again.*

∽

*You've been forgiven and declared righteous; now trust Him to
cleanse you and establish that righteousness in you by grace.*

All Things New

Truth Number 5

Jesus redeemed everything about you so that your transformation could be successful and complete.

My Dream

I've found out over the years that although God doesn't give people nightmares, the dreams he does give aren't always entirely pleasant. For me, this one was one of those dreams.

I was away, somewhere, evidently with my family and some friends. I stood across the street from where I was staying, talking with a friend of mine. The sun was shining, I knew that the beach was just behind us, and I was having a great day. The street was very busy and I glanced across it at the four- or five-story older building I was staying in. As I looked, the door to the building's rooftop garden opened and a young family member walked out. (In the dream she was probably about seven, although in real life, she was much older at the time.) I knew it was okay for her to be up there in the garden area but as I watched she started to walk past where it was safe. I knew that she was looking for her friend and not paying attention to where she was walking. I started to yell to get her attention, knowing that my voice could easily carry that far. But as I tried to yell, my voice would not come out loud and she didn't hear me. Frustrated, I began to try to get my voice to respond as I tried to find a break in the traffic to cross the street. As I tried in vain to get my voice to work, the child kept moving towards the edge of the roof, not looking down or paying attention to where the edge was. I watched in horror, trying with all my strength to scream and be heard as she walked off the edge of the roof. She seemed to hover for a split second then began falling to the street below. I woke up literally screaming.

The sheer emotional impact of this dream was so powerful that I wept for a long time.

To be continued...

PUT ON, PUT OFF

The day you received Jesus you became a new creation.

> Therefore, if anyone is in Christ, he is a new creation; old things have passed away; behold, all things have become new (2 Corinthians 5:17 NKJV).

However, you don't experience everything new when you first receive Jesus. Even though you *are* born again as a completely new creation, completely washed of your sins, you are yet to be transformed—from the inside-out—into that new creation by grace through faith.

> We all, with unveiled face, beholding the glory of the Lord, are being transformed into the same image from one degree of glory to another (2 Corinthians 3:18 ESV).

"Being saved", or "being transformed," is the progressive realization of a current reality, your complete salvation. The day you received Jesus you were completely made new, born again into a whole new life; now you must walk into that by being transformed by His grace. It's important to realize that your salvation is complete, but your transformation is progressive.

You must see the work as complete and lock your hope on the new creation and leave the old behind. Here's what you really must get. The "old you" is not "being saved." You're a new creation, the old sinful you can't be saved. He's dead. That's what baptism represents, the old you is buried with Jesus—and left in the grave—and the new you rises with Him to new life. Before you were saved, the you that was created by God and predestined before the foundation of the earth, never saw the light of day. When you were born the first time, you were born into Adam, born into sin and death, born separated from God (not one with Him or in vital union with Him). Jesus died to redeem (or buy back) the original you, the you God created in His image.

So the day you became a Christian, you became the person you were created to be. Jesus bought you back from sin, death, hell, and the grave and brought you back to your original purpose; and He paid such a complete price that even the memory of who you were, the old you, could be forever buried. That's truly getting saved—and it happened in a moment.

The new you is amazing but you still don't know all of who you are and what Jesus has made and called you to be. So now you need to grow up into who you've already been created to be. That's "being saved" or being transformed. Paul explains the process this way:

> <u>You took off your former way of life, the old self that is corrupted</u> by deceitful desires; you are being renewed in the spirit of your minds; <u>you put on the new self, the one created according to God's likeness</u> in righteousness and purity of the truth (Ephesians 4:22–24).

> …<u>you have put off the old self with its practices and have put on the new self</u>. You are being renewed in knowledge according to the image of your Creator (Colossians 3:9–10).

Knowing that you are a "new creation" and that the "old" has passed away, you put off the "old self" and put on the "new self" as you learn more and more about who you were created to be in Christ Jesus. The Lord once said to me, "I already know who I've created you to be; you just need to catch up."

It's important to see that His work is complete; you already are new. When you see yourself as the "old you" you see all of your faults, sin, pain, bad experiences, and junk. Then you have trouble seeing how God is going to deal with all the garbage and make you right. But when you see that He already dealt with all your garbage once and for all, and that your old self is dead and buried, you can set your hope on your new self and become who you were created to be.

Abraham's name was originally Abram, but God told him that he would be the father of many nations and changed his name to Abraham, which means "father of a multitude." From that moment on Abram called himself Abraham and believed that what God said about him was true. Even though Abraham was not yet the father of a multitude, he believed that He was who God said He was. Like Abraham, you believe that you are who God says you are—a new creation—and then you walk in it by grace through faith by putting off the old and putting on the new. You've been given this amazing gift—a completely new you. Now you need to unwrap it, discover it, and put it on.

But how do you put off and put on? What does that look like? Well, to start that discussion you need to connect with your Master and Teacher at work within you.

AT WORK WITHIN

Let's look again at the first verse that God used to start teaching me about His work within me, and go a little deeper.

> ... work out your own salvation with fear and trembling. For it is God who is working in you, enabling you both to desire and to work out His good purpose (Philippians 2:12–13).

The Greek word used in verse 12 for "*work out*" is *katergazomai* and it also means "accomplish" or "achieve." The Amplified version amplifies that word this way: "*work out—cultivate, carry out to the goal and fully complete—your salvation.*" Your salvation was fully accomplished for you on the cross. God isn't calling you to works, but to transformation, to walk out to completion what has already been accomplished for you.

Notice that verse 13 starts with the word, "For." You can carry your salvation through to its completion—putting off the old and putting on the new—for (because) God is at work within you causing you to *want* to do and causing you to *do* His will. I like the way the Amplified sheds light on this verse:

> [Not in your own strength] for it is God Who is all the while effectually at work in you [energizing and creating in you the power and desire] both to will and to work for His good pleasure and satisfaction and delight (Philippians 2:13 AMP).

So Jesus came to live in you by His Spirit, to teach you and cause you to *want* to act like—and *to* act like—the new creation. We've already looked at what Jeremiah (31:33–34) and Ezekiel (36:27) said about God causing you to walk in His ways, know Him, and be His obedient people; now let's look at a few more New Testament verses:

> Now may the God of peace... with the blood of the everlasting covenant, <u>equip you with all that is good to do His</u>

> will, working in us what is pleasing in His sight, through Jesus Christ. Glory belongs to Him forever and ever. Amen (Hebrews 13:20–21).

Through the everlasting covenant (Hebrews 8:7–12) God equips you to do His will and works in you what is pleasing in His sight. God didn't just make you new and say, "Now go behave!" No. He paid the price to make you new and to cause you to be fully transformed. You can put off the old and put on the new because Jesus is walking with you and working in you, teaching you, and causing you to walk as He walked and be transformed into His image. And it never stops or plateaus.

> I am sure of this, that He who started a good work in you will carry it on to completion until the day of Christ Jesus (Philippians 1:6).

The fact that you're a brand new creation and the old is gone means that nothing in your past can hold you back from being transformed. The fact that Jesus is discipling you from within and has promised to not stop, means that nothing in your present or future can hold you back either. You need to keep walking with Him, keep learning from Him, and keep believing that He's doing the work inside you no matter what. Memorize the "At Work Within" verses (Jeremiah 31:33–34; Ezekiel 36:27; Ephesians 3:20; Philippians 1:6; 2:13; Hebrews 13:20–21) and thank God constantly that His renovations are always underway.

But doesn't sin have the power to trip up your transformation?

BUT, SIN...

Your old self was a slave to sin, but your new self is righteous and naturally yielded to righteousness. You need to understand this and take hold of it by faith. Let's look at two seemingly contrary verses.

> So he took Him up and showed Him all the kingdoms of the world in a moment of time. The Devil said to Him, "I will give You their splendor and all this authority, because it has been given over to me, and I can give it to anyone I want. If You, then, will worship me, all will be Yours (Luke 4:5–7).

> The earth and everything in it, the world and its inhabitants, belong to the Lord (Psalm 24:1).

The Bible says God owns the earth and its inhabitants but the Devil claimed to have been given authority over the kingdoms of the world. In order to better understand, let's look at the background of this temptation.

The deception that the Devil tried unsuccessfully to pull on Jesus was the same one that he had used on Eve. The Devil told Eve that she could be like God, deciding for herself what was wrong and right. But as Paul said in Romans 6:16, you are slaves of whoever you obey. When Adam and Eve—who had been given authority over the earth (Genesis 1:26–28)—obeyed the Devil, they didn't become free to decide, they became slaves to sin and the Devil.

The Devil tried the same trickery with Jesus. The Devil knew that he could safely offer the kingdoms of the world because if Jesus had bowed He would have become the Devil's slave; and a slave's master owns everything the slave has. That's what happened when Adam and Eve obeyed the Devil; the kingdoms of this world were delivered to him because the people who made up those kingdoms were his slaves because of sin. The world and its inhabitants still belonged to God but the inhabitants had become slaves.

The good news is: Jesus was born without sin, He passed up the Devil's deceptive temptation and He lived His life without sin. That's why the Devil couldn't touch Jesus while He was here on earth. Jesus had no sin; therefore, the Devil had no authority over Him. In fact, just before His arrest, Jesus said this:

> ... the ruler of the world is coming. He has no power over me (John 14:30).

Jesus agreed that the Devil was the *"ruler of this world"* but made it clear that the Devil had no power over Him. Now, here's the great part! Remember the "Great Exchange"?

> He made the One who did not know sin to be sin for us, so that we might become the righteousness of God in Him (2 Corinthians 5:21).

Jesus took your place so that you could take His! You are the righteousness of God in Him. So like Jesus when He walked this earth, the Devil has no authority over you; you are no longer a slave to sin and the Devil.

> He has rescued us from the domain *(authority)* of darkness and transferred us into the Kingdom of the Son He loves (Colossians 1:13).

Because of what Jesus did, you've been rescued from the authority of the Devil. When Jesus talked about accomplishing this for you, here's how He put it:

> Jesus responded, "I assure you: <u>Everyone who commits sin is a slave to sin</u>. A slave does not remain in the household forever, but a son does remain forever. Therefore, <u>if the Son sets you free, you really will be free</u> (John 8:34–36).

You are no longer a slave to the Devil or sin. Jesus has set you free and you are a righteous son or daughter of God forever! Paul wrote extensively about this in Romans 6. I suggest you read the whole chapter, but here's a sampling:

> For we know that <u>our old self was crucified with Him in order that sin's dominion over the body may be abolished, so that we may no longer be enslaved to sin</u>... (Romans 6:6).

> For <u>sin will not rule over you</u>, because you are not under law but under grace (Romans 6:14).

Because your old sinful self is dead and buried and your new creation self is righteous and living under grace as you're being transformed, you are no longer a slave to sin; it has no power or authority to push you around or rule your life. Because you're in Christ Jesus, sin and the Devil have no authority to trip you up either.

ALL OF ME

So the next question is: what parts of you is God at work on—your character, your spirit, your mind, your will, your emotions, your thought processes, your words, your desires, your motivations, your deeds, your life, or your body? The short answer is "Yes!" to every part of you and your life. You are a new creation, not just partially new creations. Jesus rescued and redeemed every part of you: He paid for it all and He desires to lovingly transform you in every way.

> Now may the God of peace Himself <u>sanctify you completely</u>. And may <u>your spirit, soul</u>, and <u>body</u> be kept sound and blameless for the coming of our Lord Jesus Christ. He who calls you is faithful, <u>who also will do it</u> (1 Thessalonians 5:23–24).

The word "completely" here means "perfect and complete in all respects." It is not God's plan for Christ to be partially formed in parts of you, but for Him to be completely formed in all of you. God has declared every part of you righteous/sanctified/saved so that on that real foundation, He can actually transform you completely. I love verse 24 which again confirms the New Covenant: *"He who calls you is faithful, who also will do it."* He's at work within us. He's guaranteed the sanctification or transformation of your whole self and *He* will do it.

You may think that your lack of intelligence can get in the way of your transformation, that you're not able to understand His Word, or that it's just too hard for God to get through to you. Not true! That may have been who you *were*, but remember, now you're a new creation. Your mind is part of your soul and it's included in your redemption and sanctification. You have the mind of Christ (1 Corinthians 2:16) and as He is formed in you (Galatians 4:19), His mind is being formed in you as well.

Perhaps you think that your up and down emotions—your anger or your depression, etc.—are too much for you to overcome and move beyond. No, you're a new creation, and by grace through faith the Holy Spirit is at work in you producing new Christlike fruit in your emotions.

> But the fruit of the Spirit is love, joy, peace, patience, kindness, goodness, faith, gentleness, self-control (Galatians 5:22–23).

Have you ever thought that this spiritual fruit is something that you need to struggle to produce or display, but not necessarily feel on the inside? No. This fruit is who you *are* and therefore who you're being transformed into. More and more as I'm transformed, that list describes how I feel on the inside and that automatically affects my behavior. Grape vines naturally produce grapes; and new creations, who are created in God's image, naturally yield spiritual fruit.

If you feel like you're just too lazy or that your desire for other things will hold you back, He will work in you and cause you to want to do and to do His will (Philippians 2:13) as you trust Him. Moses even prophesied about the transformation of your motivations:

> The LORD your <u>God will circumcise your heart</u> and the hearts of your descendants, and you will love Him with <u>all your heart and all your soul</u>, so that you will live (Deuteronomy 30:6).

Moses prophesied that God would change your hearts (the new creation) so that you *will* love God with all your heart and all your soul. How many times have you felt like you've fallen short of loving God with all that is within you? Well, that amazing prophecy involves *"all your heart and all your soul"* which includes your mind, thoughts, will, emotions, desires, and motivations. What amazing love and grace! God gently renews and transforms you in love so that you are then able to truly love and be loved.

How about attitude? Perhaps you think you're just too belligerent or hard-headed for the Lord to change you. No, God asks you to have the same attitude as Jesus had (Philippians 2:5), so that means it's possible for you to have that. As a new creation, His attitude is your attitude and He's ready to form that in you. God said, *"I will remove your heart of stone and give you a heart of flesh"* (Ezekiel 36:26).

But how about your body?

YOUR BODY

Sometimes you may think that you'd be okay if it wasn't for that nasty earth-suit that keeps dragging you off in the wrong direction. But Paul wrote, *"... may your spirit, soul, and <u>body</u> be kept sound and blameless"* (1 Thessalonians 5:23). In order for God to *"keep"* your body sound and blameless, He must have first "made" it sound and blameless in Christ as part of the new creation.

Paul wrote:

> <u>The body is not for sexual immorality but for the Lord, and the Lord for the body</u>.... <u>Don't you know that your bodies are a part of Christ's body</u>? (1 Corinthians 6:13, 15).

<u>Do you not know that your body is a sanctuary of the Holy Spirit</u> who is in you, whom you have from God? You are not your own, <u>for you were bought at a price. Therefore glorify God in your body</u> (1 Corinthians 6:19–20).

Your body was included in your redemption: The body is *"for the Lord, and the Lord for the Body"* because He bought/redeemed it. It's His. Paul says *"You are not your own, for you were bought at a price,"* and the scripture's context is about the body, so the *"you"* here clearly includes the body.

Your body is the sanctuary of the Holy Spirit because it was bought and sanctified by Jesus. Therefore we as Christians can *"glorify God in our bodies"* because they are part of the new creation and the Holy Spirit is at work within them. When the Bible teaches that God is at work within you, you tend to get confused and think that He's working only in your inner self. No, God created "you" spirit, soul, and body and He's at work within "you," spirit, soul, and body.

> Now if Christ is in you, <u>the body is dead because of sin</u>, but the Spirit is life because of righteousness. And if the Spirit of Him who raised Jesus from the dead lives in you, <u>then He who raised Christ from the dead will also bring your mortal bodies to life through His Spirit</u> who lives in you (Romans 8:10–11).

These verses are not talking about the future resurrection, they are talking about our bodies now. Look at the next verse; it clearly puts Paul's teaching in the context of this life.

> So then, brothers, we are not obligated to the flesh to live according to the flesh … (Romans 8:12).

Your unredeemed body—along with your old spirit and soul—was buried in Christ when you accepted your salvation. The body you now have—although it looks the same—is considered by God to be redeemed, sanctified, and brought to life by the Spirit. The body you had was fallen; the body you have now is Christ's and is the temple of the Holy Spirit. Your new body is like Christ's sinless body that He had here on earth, and your future glorified body will be like Christ's current glorified body. Your body is included in "saved," "being saved," and "will be saved."

What's really interesting about these verses is the meaning behind the two different Greek words Paul uses. In the Greek the word *soma* means "body" or your physical bodies. The Greek word *sarx* can mean "body" but most often it means "flesh," your sinful flesh. The vast majority of times the word *sarx* is used in the New Testament it's referring to your old, fallen self (spirit, soul, and body) with its evil desires and tendencies.

In Romans 8:10–11 Paul uses the word *soma* when he says that *"the body (soma) is dead because of sin"* and *"bring your mortal bodies (soma) to life through His Spirit."* Then in verse 12 he uses the word *sarx*: *"So then, brothers, we are not obligated to the flesh (sarx) to live according to the flesh (sarx)"*. When you look at the difference in these words it becomes clear what Paul is saying: because your physical bodies are part of the new creation—and indwelt and empowered by the Holy Spirit—you no longer have to yield to the old sinful self.

> Therefore, brothers, by the mercies of God, I urge you to <u>present your bodies</u> as a living sacrifice, <u>holy and pleasing to God</u>; this is your spiritual worship (Romans 12:1).

You can present your body as *"holy and pleasing to God"* because it has been redeemed.

> For we know that our <u>old self was crucified with Him in order that sin's dominion over the body may be abolished</u>... (Romans 6:6).

You have been set free from sin because the old self is dead—spirit, soul, and body—and you are a new creation. The old desires may come knocking but those desires are no longer part of who you are. Your old self and its desires no longer have the authority to use your body to lead you where you don't want to go.

Ask the Father to help you see yourself as a new creation—completely new and absolutely free from sin. Then trust that God is powerfully at work within you, causing you to want to do, and to do, His good pleasure. Even if sometimes you feel like it's not working, keep believing. Faith is believing to be true what you don't yet see and feel. Yes, your transformation is progressive, but what I've found is, the more I focus on and believe that I already *am* the new creation—in any area—the faster my transformation takes place. Transformation is the art of discovering, believing, and walking in who God has already declared you to be.

When you've blown it, it's important to remember who you *are* because your thoughts will try and convince you that you're scum, that God is not happy, and that transformation won't work for you. Call each of those thoughts lies and speak God's truth. Slipping up and sinning doesn't mean you're not a new creation; it just means that you're growing.

Nothing about yourself has been left out of your redemption so nothing can hold you back from being transformed in every area. If you see that any part of your life is not lining up to the image of Jesus, then pray and trust Him to transform you. For some things in your life, the transformation will happen quickly. For other things, you'll need to stay at it for a while, cooperating with God's "at work within" process.

SPIRIT-LED CHANGE

You can trust God to move you forward one issue at a time (it is a relationship), but ultimately it is your loving Master—who knows you best—who manages your transformation. As you cooperate it'll amaze you how change that you weren't even thinking about will happen. Sometimes God does things so deep within you you're not sure what happened, but you know you're different; other times He'll work with you in the process and teach you what He's doing while He's changing you.

When the Lord is teaching you the Holy Spirit will often use your conscience and His "still small voice" (1 Kings 19:12 NKJV) within you to give you a nudge concerning things that He's working on. For example, you may have raised your voice or responded impatiently to someone and afterwards you feel God's Spirit inside you nudge you to apologize.

Now that you're starting to understand transformation by grace the Holy Spirit's work inside you will increase. Why? Before when you thought that you had to change yourself, God's Spirit would not be aggressive in His prodding because it would often just result in you doubling your efforts, then failing, and feeling condemned. But when you understand the process, God's Spirit will step things up because you know that He is merely pointing out what *He is doing* in you and how He wants you to cooperate.

Whenever the Spirit prompts me or the Lord speaks to me, I stop and do two simple things: I say, "Yes! That's who I am!" then I ask Him to work it in me. Smile every time this happens because when the Spirit takes on a "Temple Improvement" project He provides His own materials and tools and always completes the job. The more you cooperate with God, the easier it gets and actually, the more fun it is. Stop and invite the Holy Spirit to take His temple improvement projects to the next level in you.

There's no part of you that hasn't been made new; but you may wonder, "How about my life?"

THE TRANSFORMED LIFE

The most effective way to change your life is to change you—not your spouse, job, friends, church, or circumstances, but *you*. Really! When you let Jesus transform you, your life will change.

For example, you can attend marriage conferences, get counseling and read a marriage book a week yet only see nominal changes in your relationship. Learning tips and principles are great, but if old-self things like anger, impatience, and selfishness still dominate you, you're just applying whitewash. However, if you're putting off the old self and putting on the new, then the real problem—your old selves—is being dealt with and a new-creation love relationship can blossom.

My wife and I don't fight. We don't always agree, but when we disagree, we work things out lovingly. We use some of the tips we've learned from great Christian books but what really makes the difference is the work Jesus is doing within us. We have an amazing relationship that's constantly getting better not because we double up on our efforts to be nice, but because God is transforming us into the kind, giving, loving, patient, forgiving people he created us to be. God's plan for transforming Christian marriage is to transform each one of the partners in a marriage.

You can see that the same is true in every area of your life. The more you're transformed into His image, the more you walk with Him, hear Him, and receive His wisdom and direction—and the more your relationships grow and opportunities open. You become better in everything you do, even at handling problems and obstacles and moving out in faith, and as you do, His blessings come. Your life changes as you become the kind of person who lives and works in order to love and give. As you become who God made you to be, you stop "trying" to make your life "appear" Christian and blessed by God, and it actually becomes that as you walk with Him.

My dream continued…

In my dream I watched helplessly while a young family member walked off the top of a building. Although what I had witnessed was horrific, it hadn't actually happened. It was only a dream. Yet, I felt like I had actually experienced it.

As I prayed, peace came then something that had been missing from my dream struck me: *I hadn't prayed*. As I became more settled, I remembered that I had been struggling recently in a few situations when counseling others. In one case, I was having a difficult time seeing how this person could be transformed and experience the "new them" and a "new life." Then the meaning of the dream came to me like a flood. The young girl represented each one of God's children and I felt the overwhelming love He has for each one. However, the helplessness I felt was mine. Jesus has already paid the price and unlike me, He is not powerless to help. You can't change anyone, but He can transform everyone.

God never gives up on you and is always able to rescue, heal, restore, and transform no matter what has happened: and He wants to do it! Don't entertain the enemy when he's trying to convince you that you, and/or someone you know, has already walked off the edge or "it's too late" or "you've gone too far." You've been completely redeemed, made new in every way, and your transformation is guaranteed. Nothing can get in your way.

Pray this prayer and if you feel the need, add your own words at any point.

> "Thank You, Father, for making me a new creation—spirit, soul, and body, which includes all of me. Thank You that the old me is dead and the new me—which You created in the image of Jesus—is now alive in Him. Thank You for giving me a new heart, a new spirit, the mind of Christ, and for filling me with Your Holy Spirit and making me a partaker of Your divine

nature. Thank You for making me righteous and for sanctifying me completely. Jesus, please teach me how to put off the old self and put on the new self, and cause me to cooperate with and trust You as You work powerfully within me. Thank You for redeeming the true and real me, the *me* You created me to be. Cause me to live in the freedom that You paid for and transform me from glory to glory into Your image."

Next let's look at the essential role that God's Word and the renewing of your minds, play in your transformation.

POWER POINTS FROM TRUTH NUMBER 5
Quotes for Sharing on Social Media

Salvation is complete, but your transformation is progressive.

∽

The "old you" is not "being saved." You're a new creation, the old sinful you can't be saved. He's dead.

∽

Jesus died to redeem (or buy back) the original you, the you God created in His image.

∽

Jesus bought you back from sin, death, hell, and the grave and brought you back to your original purpose;

∽

Like Abraham, you believe that you are who God says you are—a new creation—and then you walk in it by grace through faith

*You've been given this amazing gift—a completely new you.
Now you need to unwrap it, discover it, and put it on.*

∽

*God isn't calling you to works, but to transformation, to walk out
to completion what has already been accomplished for you.*

∽

*Your old self was a slave to sin, but your new self is
righteous and naturally yielded to righteousness.*

∽

*You are the righteousness of God in Him. So like Jesus when
He walked this earth, the Devil has no authority over you.*

∽

*You are no longer a slave to the Devil or sin. Jesus has set you
free and you are a righteous son or daughter of God forever!*

∽

*Jesus rescued and redeemed every part of you: He paid for it all
and He desires to lovingly transform you in every way.*

∽

*It is not God's plan for Christ to be partially formed in parts
of you, but for Him to be completely formed in all of you.*

∽

*You have the mind of Christ and as He is formed in you
(Galatians 4:19), His mind is being formed in you as well.*

∽

*Grape vines naturally produce grapes; and new creations,
who are created in God's image, naturally yield spiritual fruit.*

*God gently renews and transforms you in love so that
you are then able to truly love and be loved.*

*Your body is the sanctuary of the Holy Spirit because
it was bought and sanctified by Jesus.*

*God created "you," spirit, soul, and body and
He's at work within "you," spirit, soul, and body.*

*The body you had was fallen; the body you have now
is Christ's and is the temple of the Holy Spirit.*

*You can present your body as "holy and pleasing
to God" because it has been redeemed.*

*You have been set free from sin because the old self is dead
—spirit, soul, and body—and you are a new creation.*

*Your old self and its desires no longer have the authority
to use your body to lead you where you don't want to go.*

*Trust that God is powerfully at work within you,
causing you to want to do, and to do, His good pleasure.*

*Slipping up and sinning doesn't mean you're not a new
creation; it just means that you're growing.*

*Nothing about yourself has been left out of your redemption so
nothing can hold you back from being transformed in every area.*

∼

*When the Spirit takes on a "Temple Improvement" project
He provides His own materials and tools and always completes the job.*

∼

*The most effective way to change your life is to change you—
not your spouse, job, friends, church, or circumstances, but* you.

∼

*God's plan for transforming Christian marriage is to
transform each one of the partners in a marriage.*

∼

*Your life changes as you become the kind of person
who lives and works in order to love and give.*

∼

You can't change anyone, but He can transform everyone.

∼

*God never gives up on you and is always able to rescue, heal,
restore, and transform no matter what has happened.*

∼

*You've been completely redeemed, made new in every way,
and your transformation is guaranteed.
Nothing can get in your way.*

The Renewing of Your Mind

Truth Number 6
Having your mind renewed with God's Word is an essential part of your transformation.

My wife's dream...

She was standing beside an expanse of lawn looking across it to the other side where she needed to be. Many women all dressed in black robes occupied the lawn. She knew that they were not women of faith but, in fact, were set against the faith. Although they were taking no notice of her now, she was sure that they would not be very friendly when she attempted to cross the lawn.

She braced herself, stepped on the grass and started to head towards her goal. As anticipated, the closest woman in black turned, looked right at her then headed towards her with a smile on her face. My wife knew the smile was not genuine. As the woman approached, my wife instinctively felt God's authority and put her hand up, palm out, and signaled for her opponent to stop. "No!" She commanded. The woman in black suddenly stopped, but then another woman in black turned around and also began to approach her. My wife did the same with this woman, and the next, and the next, as each took turns trying to approach. With each "No!" her confidence increased and her hand moved more quickly from woman to woman. As one of the last women headed towards her, my wife's confidence was so strong, she knew she didn't even have to say anything. She just snapped her fingers and the woman fell helplessly to the ground. My wife woke up and knew instantly what the dream meant.

To be continued...

THE PURPOSE AND POWER OF GOD'S WORD

This section is about the renewing of your minds, and since God uses His Word in that process, we're going to look first at what the Bible teaches about its own role in your transformation. In the second half of this section we'll examine how you are to interact with God's Word to have your mind renewed.

God's Word is alive and powerful (Hebrews 4:12). In fact, God's Word contains the power in itself to accomplish what God has purposed and declared.

> …My word that comes from My mouth will not return to Me empty, but it will accomplish what I please and will prosper in what I send it to do" (Isaiah 55:11).

The context of this verse is clearest in verse 3 of Isaiah 55, which says, "*I will make an everlasting covenant with you.*" In the same chapter the Holy Spirit encourages "*everyone who is thirsty*" to "*come to the water*" and tells you that God will have "*compassion*" on you and "*freely forgive.*" The verses surrounding verse 11 about God's Word accomplishing its purpose show you that the purpose of God's powerful Word is to explain, facilitate, and cause your New Covenant transformation. God's vision for humanity is to make you in His image and likeness, and His Word was given to you to accomplish that purpose.

The Bible is God's Word and He spoke it and had men write it down, not only to reveal Himself and His purpose for humanity—"*Let Us make man in our image and likeness*"—but also to give you the power and how-to knowledge necessary to transform you.

Paul taught about the power and purpose of God's Word as well.

> …from childhood you have known the sacred Scriptures, <u>which are able to give you wisdom for salvation through faith in Christ Jesus</u>. All Scripture is inspired by God and is profitable for teaching, for rebuking, for correcting, <u>for training in righteousness, so that the man of God may be complete</u>, equipped for every good work (2 Timothy 3:15–17).

Paul states God's purpose for giving you the Scriptures is "*to give you wisdom for salvation*," and again, "*so that the man of God may be complete*." The word translated "*complete*" means "perfect." God designed and empowered His Word to achieve His goal: your transformation into His image in Christ Jesus. His Word gives you the wisdom, promises, and how-to knowledge—and all of the power and resources of heaven show up to make what God spoke happen when you believe it.

The Gospel is the core message of the entire Bible, and Paul said:

> For I am not ashamed of the gospel, because it is God's power for salvation to everyone who believes, first to the Jew, and also to the Greek (Romans 1:16; see also 1 Corinthians 1:18).

Just as God said, "*Let there be light*" and light came into being, as you learn, believe, and embrace His Word, you will be transformed into Christ's image. Jesus prayed, "*Sanctify them by the truth; Your word is truth*" (John 17:17). God's Word sanctifies you because it has the power in itself to accomplish God's purpose, your transformation.

> This is why we constantly thank God, because when you received the message about God that you heard from us, you welcomed it not as a human message, but as it truly is, the message of God, which also works effectively in you believers (1 Thessalonians 2:13).

When you sit with the Teacher and He opens the Word to you and writes it on your heart, the transforming power that God invested in His Word literally "*works effectively in you*" and starts helping you put off and put on. Ever got lost in a good book? You are literally meant to lose yourself in the Good Book and come out transformed.

PLUGGING INTO GOD'S WORD

If you inherited a fortune from a long-lost relative but never found out about it, you'd never know to pick it up. If you did find out, the first thing you'd need to do is read the will so you'd know what was yours. Jesus has made *much* available for you and the understanding of what you've been given is in His Word (2 Peter 1:3). In order to grow into all God created you to be, you need to get into the Book He designed to facilitate and empower your journey.

Paul also taught that knowing is a prerequisite to growing:

> So faith comes from what is heard, and what is heard comes through the message about Christ (Romans 10:17).

Learning what God did for you in Christ Jesus gives birth to hope; then you can receive it by grace through faith. I like the way James put it:

> Therefore, ridding yourselves of all moral filth and evil, <u>humbly receive the implanted word, which is able to save you</u> (James 1:21).

The word translated "*ridding yourselves*" would be better translated "putting off." You need to humbly receive God's Word, which is able to save you ("being saved") by informing you—so you know what to put off and put on—and empowering you to do it. The word "*implanted*" paints such a great picture. Jeremiah prophesied that in the New Covenant God would place His Word within you *and* write it on your heart (31:33). As you learn God's Word He plants it within you and Jesus, your Teacher, causes you to understand it and be transformed by it.

Jesus taught that you are not to worry or be anxious about your physical needs (Matthew 6:25–34) or to get caught up with the cares of this life (Matthew 13:22). He taught you to not let your heart be troubled or fearful (John 14:27). He also taught you, through Paul, to not be anxious about anything (Philippians 4:6), and through Peter that you are to cast your cares onto Him (1 Peter 5:7). From these verses you can see that as a new creation you're called to be worry-free; therefore God has already provided you with all you need in Christ to walk in it and His very Words on the topic carry the power to transform you into a worry-free person.

If you haven't already done it, why not start with this: confess your worries and fears to the Lord and ask Him to set you free from them. Then ask Him to teach you, work within you, and transform you into His image in this area. Read, study, and memorize a few "worry-free" verses and choose to believe that your new self doesn't worry or get anxious about anything but instead prays about everything and trusts God in everything.

You may, of course, need to look up verses about what you've been worried about. If you're perplexed about finances you'll need to get into the Word and trust Jesus to teach you what God promises about meeting your needs and blessing you. Then every time the Holy Spirit nudges you in the middle of your worried thoughts, thank Him and put off the old you and put on the new you by quoting the verses you memorized—concerning worry and the thing you are being tempted to worry about. Take a break and pray right now, then put aside some time to study the topic and let Jesus teach you. Then stick with it and watch the Lord, the Spirit, and the Word work in you.

I've done this and the Lord continues to take me deeper and deeper into His peace. Sometimes I find myself so worry free that if I was a worrier, it would be worrisome. All joking aside, it's an amazing way to live your life and you'll find, as I did, that faith blossoms in a worry-free heart. This life will always provide the opportunities to worry but by His grace, the power of His mighty Word, and His work within you, you can trust Him instead.

When you read and study God's Word looking for personal transformation opportunities like "being worry free" it gets exciting. Instead of being challenged or discouraged by trying to "live up to" God's Word, you dive into it, searching for hidden treasure, looking for who you are and what God has already given you in Christ Jesus (Ephesians 1:18–19). God's Word is His treasure map to the new creation.

Whatever you're struggling with, the grace and power you need has already been provided to transform you in that area of your life. But it's hidden in the "*knowledge of Him*," hidden in Christ and His Word. Ask Jesus to teach you and transform you, dust off your Bible, and start reading and studying what it says about your area of struggle. Persevere in your study, trusting Jesus to guide and teach you. Once you know what God's Word teaches on the topic, memorize the scriptures and start using them to "put off" and "put on." Before God's Word can start working in you, you need to get into it and let it get into you.

Learning from His Word isn't hard. Since He's called you to it, He'll work it in you by grace. Jesus has promised to teach you and He'll even teach you how to read and study His Word with Him. He put the whole system together in such a way that each of His children can learn from Him through His Word.

> At that time Jesus said, "I praise You, Father, Lord of heaven and earth, because You have hidden these things from the wise and learned <u>and revealed them to infants</u> (Matthew 11:25).

God has used me as a prime example of this. I'm just an average guy with no special training in anything. Yet I know that by His grace I'm taught by Jesus and the more I've trusted Him, the more He's taught me. You need to remember that Jesus picked very ordinary guys to be His Disciples. If you needed to be extraordinary in any way in order to learn His Word, then it wouldn't be by grace.

Jesus teaches me every day. But He does so when I'm in His Word. The times He teaches me without my Bible open in front of me, He uses the Bible that I've stored in my heart (John 14:26) as His jumping-off point. Why does He use His Word? Because your own thoughts can mislead you. Even when you're sincere you can be sincerely wrong. When God reveals truth to me I dig deeper, looking at related verses, commentaries, the original language, etc., trusting Jesus to teach me how to study His Word and to confirm what He's shown me. If the Bible doesn't support what I thought, I forget it. If it is confirmed in His Word, I ask Jesus to write it in my heart and transform me with it.

If you struggle with reading and studying God's Word or making time for it, that's covered by grace as well. There were times I struggled in this area. However, as I started to rely on the Master and His grace to draw me into His Word and teach me, my time in the Bible and my love for it increased dramatically. Now I honestly have no trouble picking it up and getting into it. It's putting it back down that I sometimes have difficulty with.

God has given you His Word, and He's provided you with Jesus as your Teacher. He's promised to reveal its truths to you and to set you free and transform you and your life by His truth. Your responsibility is to receive these incredible gifts by grace through faith and start devouring His Word (Jeremiah 15:16).

RENEWING THE MIND

Now we need to look at the renewing of your mind and how that interconnects with the grace-mechanics of your transformation. Romans 12:2 is the classic verse about renewing your mind, but let's start by looking at the verse just *before* it.

> Therefore, brothers, by the mercies of God, I urge you to present your bodies as a living sacrifice, holy and pleasing to God; this is your spiritual worship (Romans 12:1).

Under the Old Covenant each animal offered as a sacrifice had to be inspected because it had to be perfect without defect or blemish. Jesus was the perfect lamb, *"without defect or blemish"* (1 Peter 1:19) and you are to be transformed into His image. Peter wrote that you are to *"make every effort to be found at peace with Him without spot or blemish"* (2 Peter 3:14). Here Paul wrote, *"I urge you to present your bodies as a living sacrifice, holy and pleasing to God."* Your salvation is complete in Christ—you are a new creation—but your transformation is progressive. The goal of your transformation is to grow into His perfect, holy, and blameless image. Paul calls this your *"spiritual worship."* You gratefully respond to your amazing salvation by walking out your transformation with Jesus.

In the next verse Paul tells you how to walk out your transformation so that you can present yourself holy and pleasing to God.

> Do not be conformed to this age, but be transformed by the renewing of your mind, so that you may discern what is the good, pleasing, and perfect will of God (Romans 12:2).

When you consume the Word, trusting the Teacher to teach you and write it on your heart, your mind is renewed and His Spirit and the power of His Word transform you. As your mind is renewed you start to think like God thinks and it becomes easier to discern what His will is and live it. Although your Teacher drives the mind-renewing process, you have a cooperative part to play. Let's look at a simple example of how that works.

You start by reading the Word and learning God's will. Jesus said:

> "You have heard that it was said, Do not commit adultery. But I tell you, everyone who looks at a woman to lust for her has already committed adultery with her in his heart" (Matthew 5:27–28).

Jesus didn't teach this so that you could spend your life fighting wayward thoughts. He taught it so that you'd know what the new creation looks like and you could be transformed. When I was newly saved and learned this scripture I knew my thinking needed to change in this area. So I memorized two scriptures, which to start with, I quoted many, many times a day. They were one above and the following:

> Everyone who has been born of God does not sin, because... he is not able to sin, because he has been born of God (1 John 3:9).

Each time a temptation would come to look at a woman and think anything below God's standard, I would pray, "Lord, You said that to look at a woman lustfully is sin and I'm born of God and I do not sin." I simply put on the new me. It was a struggle at first but after awhile it got easier and easier. Soon those kind of thoughts were no longer a problem and whenever they did present themselves, I quickly squashed them like pesky mosquitoes. Why did it become easier? I was cooperating with God's process, trusting Him and obediently presenting myself before Him as a living sacrifice. So the Holy Spirit and the divine power invested in God's Word went to work and transformed me in this area by grace.

It wasn't just my thoughts that were being changed. I was being changed, from the inside-out into the new creation God made me to be. I started out thinking that I needed to merely change a habit or a thought pattern, but the result was so much bigger. In the absence of the old thoughts I started thinking of every woman as a sister, of protecting them, praying for them, caring for them, and being truly interested in their wellbeing. I presented myself as a living sacrifice and the Holy Spirit used the Word and transformed me.

When discussing this issue in the church, we sometimes tell women that it's their responsibility to dress "modestly" so that they don't cause the men in the church to stumble. Our focus is in the wrong place. What happens when those men are not at church, where the women have no dress code? Or when late night television and inappropriate websites are available to them? I agree that women should not be scantily clad, but not for the men's sake but for their own. Christian men need to have their minds renewed and let Jesus transform them into His image.

> Therefore, I say this and testify in the Lord: <u>You should no longer walk as the Gentiles walk, in the futility of their thoughts</u>. They are darkened in their understanding, excluded from the life of God, because of the ignorance that is in them and because of the hardness of their hearts. They became callous <u>and gave themselves</u> over to promiscuity for the practice of every kind of impurity with a desire for more and more (Ephesians 4:17–19).

Paul states that you should no longer walk in the futility of your thoughts as unsaved people do. Why? Because two things exclude people *"from the life of God"*—ignorance and a hard heart. Before you had your mind renewed, your thoughts were a sewer of misconception, untruth, selfishness, and darkness. Although your heart is now made new in Christ, ignorance of His Word can continue to exclude you *"from the life of God."* What Paul says next shows how powerful your thoughts can be: *"They… gave themselves over…"* You end up giving yourself over to what you chose to think about. You can't walk in the life God has for you if you're ignorant of His Word and you're thinking the futile thoughts of this world.

Paul goes on to show you how to change the way you think.

> But that is not how you learned about the Messiah, assuming you heard about Him and were taught by Him, because the truth is in Jesus. You took off your former way of life, the old self that is corrupted by deceitful desires; you are being renewed in the spirit of your minds; you put on the new self, the one created according to God's likeness in righteousness and purity of the truth (Ephesians 4:20–24).

When you were saved your old self, which was *"corrupted by deceitful desires,"* was crucified and buried with Christ; but in order to walk that change out you must be *"renewed in the spirit of [your] minds."* So you get into His Word and discover who you are as a new creation and you use His Word to cooperate with Jesus in the renewing of your mind. You do that by putting off old thoughts and thought patterns and putting on the new ones. The transformation of your thoughts leads to transformation in your words and actions as God's Word goes to work in you.

Here are a few verses that supply you with practical examples:

> But now you must also put away all the following: anger, wrath, malice, slander, and filthy language from your mouth. Do not lie to one another, <u>since you have put off the old self with its practices and have put on the new self. You are being renewed in knowledge according to the image of your Creator</u> (Colossians 3:8–10).

You find out from these verses that any issues your old self had with anger, wrath, malice, slander, filthy language, and lying are to be put away. If you're dealing with any of theses issues, memorize these verses. But don't just treat the negative. If you're dealing with anger, pair these verses with verses about the fruit of the Spirit (Galatians 5:22–23) and determine to become patient, gentle, and kind, just like your Master. If you have an issue with unedifying words coming out of your mouth, memorize these verses, together with Ephesians 4:29, and let God transform you so that all of your words are always helpful and build others up.

Every time your thoughts or behavior head back into old-self territory quote and pray the Word—presenting yourself as a living sacrifice—and determine to put off the old self and put on the new. Declare, "That's *not* who I am!" As you trust Him and walk this out, you'll be amazed at what happens on the inside. Jesus will teach you a new way of thinking and acting and the Holy Spirit will take the power of God's Word, work within you, and transform you into the new creation. Transformation isn't anger management. It's getting angry at your old management and having your new management formed in you.

Consume God's Word not just to be informed but to be transformed.

STRONGHOLDS

Renewing your mind is not just about changing the way you think about some things. You've been given the mind of Christ and you're called to put it on so that you end up thinking like He does in everything.

> Be careful that no one takes you captive through philosophy and empty deceit based on human tradition... and not based on Christ (Colossians 2:8; see also Philippians 2:5).

When Eve listened to the serpent, she questioned God's love and trustworthiness and sent the world into a tailspin of trying to discern truth apart from God. She was *"taken captive"* and the world is still full of fruitless questioning and searching. In Christ, you are called to simply trust that the One who created everything knows how it all works and that He'll teach you.

> ...the weapons of our warfare are not worldly, but are powerful through God for the demolition of strongholds. We demolish arguments and every high-minded thing that is raised up against the knowledge of God, taking every thought captive to obey Christ (2 Corinthians 10:3–5).

As you embark on this journey you'll find that there are strongholds of thought in your mind—ways of established thinking that are anchored to past experiences or emotions—that won't move easily. You need to decide to put away your old way of thinking and agree with God's Word in everything, *"taking every thought captive to obey Christ"* and *"humbly receiving the implanted Word."* As you do, Jesus will teach you His Word and build new strongholds of understanding in you that will replace the old ones. For you to be fully transformed your thinking needs to be fully transformed; to put on Christ you need to take on the mind of Christ.

In my experience, the biggest mental stronghold lies in the area of accepting who I am as a new creation. Likewise, the world, the Devil, and your old self will want to remind you of your failures, shortcomings, sins, and mistakes and tell you that you're not worthy to be all God declares you to be. You must allow God's Word to demolish these strongholds.

As I'm writing this, God gave me a picture. I saw a proverbial family picture wall in heaven with all of the pictures of God's children wonderfully and individually framed, and proudly displayed on it. As I looked at the wall, I saw many of His children finding their own picture and removing it from the wall. That's what you do when you don't believe what He says about you and count yourself somehow unworthy or unable to receive all Christ Jesus done for you. God is saying, "Please stop taking your picture off the family wall. I love you and you belong there!" If you believe that God's Word is true, then you must believe that what it says about you is true.

Jesus lovingly, patiently teaches and transforms you; you can trust Him to disciple you and to demolish even the biggest strongholds. Choose to trust Him and His Word and ask Him to draw you into the Bible and transform you by conducting a complete one-thought-at-a-time renovation of your mind.

RANDOM THOUGHTS

Remember this very important truth: not every thought that comes into your mind represents who you are. During the process of renewing your mind—and even sometimes long after your mind has been renewed in a certain area—a thought from your old self will do a drive-by shooting in your brain. This is a normal part of the process. You can't move from one way of thinking to another without overlap. Your mind is "being" renewed. It's a process. You are defined by the thoughts you choose and chew on, not by all the ones that float through.

> So if you have been raised with the Messiah, <u>seek what is above</u>, where the Messiah is, seated at the right hand of God. <u>Set your minds</u> on what is above, not on what is on the earth (Colossians 3:1–3).

The original language for "*set your minds*" means to exercise your mind and make a choice. If you automatically thought the way you should, the Holy Spirit wouldn't be telling you to "*seek what is above*" and to "*set your minds.*" God gave you a brain that could think through everything and make choices out of that thought process. So your "thinking through" and "passing through" thoughts are not who you are. It's your "conclusion" thoughts or the ones you decide to "set our mind on" that begin to define you.

THINKING LIKE GOD

When Eve chose to eat the fruit, she decided to figure life out for herself apart from God. The way this world currently thinks and operates is the result of that messed-up quest.

> "No! You will not die," the serpent said to the woman. "In fact, God knows that when you eat it your eyes will be opened and you will be like God, knowing good and evil" (Genesis 3:4–5).

You were created to be God's child, to be one with Him, walk with Him and to look like, think like, and act like Him. In this world you often have difficulty with the idea of trusting God and surrendering yourself to His will. Your mind screams, "I'm an individual! I can figure it out for myself! No one is going to tell me what to do! I'm nobody's brainless puppet!" That's basically the same argument that the devil used on Eve just before she became *his* brainless puppet. The whole argument is based on the idea that each of you are independent individuals who do as you please and rise and fall on your own choices and merits, responsible for only yourself. That's not who God is or who He created you to be. That's who the Devil is.

God is Father, Son, and Holy Spirit in loving, unified coexistence and He created you to be one with the triune God and with each other. In order for that to work you need to value, love, trust, and submit to one another. Satan wants you imitating him, living in selfish codependency. God wants you imitating Him, living in loving interdependence.

> Therefore, be imitators of God, as dearly loved children (Ephesians 5:1).

God doesn't call you to trust Him and yield to this process so that you can be His slaves but so that you can learn to think like He does, be transformed into His image, and walk in unselfish loving oneness with Him and each other, as His children.

My wife's dream continued…

As she stepped onto and crossed the lawn towards her goal, women of bad intent whose purpose was to stop her, came at her. When she woke up she knew that the women in black represented thoughts and thought patterns that had been trying to keep her from moving forward in her transformation. God was showing her what she needed to do. In the following days as soon as one of these thoughts would rise up, she would immediately speak out "No!"—sometimes even using the hand gesture she had used in the dream. I would see and hear her doing it throughout the day.

God was encouraging her in her efforts to—as she so wonderfully puts it—"practice right thinking." I love that phrase because as we've discussed, it is God who renews your mind. But you are called to cooperate by learning God's truth and applying it to your thoughts; that can aptly be called "practicing right thinking."

What was illustrated in the dream is that each time you set out to cooperate with God in the renewal of your mind, a certain process ensues. First, as soon as you learn something new from His Word and embark on the journey, it seems that the old thoughts (represented by the women in black) become relentless and persistent. However, as you stay at it, the power of God's Word and the Holy Spirit within you will empower the process. Soon you'll notice that the wrong thoughts visit less and less and when they do, they are obliterated more easily.

You were never meant to merely read and know God's Word; He gave it to you so that you would become transformed by it. Remember that every time you open it. I currently have several mind-renewal projects underway and the grace-transformation I'm seeing as I cooperate with God's process is amazing.

Stop and pray; talk with God about what you've learned in this section. If you've never used God's Word to intentionally cooperate with the renewing of your mind, ask Him to work this in you and help you get started. Whether this is your first time or you've already been doing this for years, ask Him to help you pick a topic and get moving.

You've probably noticed that all through this book I've encouraged you to pray about everything. Prayer is an essential part of your transformation because the core of Christianity is your relationship with God, your Father, Master, and Counselor. In the next section we focus on that relationship and how to pray through your transformation.

POWER POINTS FROM TRUTH NUMBER 6
Quotes for Sharing on Social Media

God's Word contains the power in itself to accomplish what God has purposed and declared.

God designed and empowered His Word to achieve His goal: your transformation into His image in Christ Jesus.

All of the power and resources of heaven show up to make what God spoke happen when you believe it.

God's Word sanctifies you because it has the power in itself to accomplish God's purpose, your transformation.

Ever got lost in a good book? You are literally meant to lose yourself in the Good Book and come out transformed.

Knowing is a prerequisite to growing.

Learning what God did for you in Christ Jesus gives birth to hope; then you can receive it by grace through faith.

*As you learn God's Word He plants it within you and Jesus,
your Teacher, causes you to understand it and be transformed by it.*

∼

*Sometimes I find myself so worry free that
if I was a worrier, it would be worrisome.*

∼

Faith blossoms in a worry-free heart.

∼

God's Word is His treasure map to the new creation.

∼

*Before God's Word can start working in you,
you need to get into it and let it get into you.*

∼

*Jesus has promised to teach you and He'll even teach you
how to read and study His Word with Him.*

∼

*If you needed to be extraordinary in any way in order
to learn His Word, then it wouldn't be by grace.*

∼

*Gratefully respond to your amazing salvation
by walking out your transformation with Jesus.*

∼

*As your mind is renewed you start to think like God thinks and
it becomes easier to discern what His will is and live it.*

You can't walk in the life God has for you if you're ignorant of His Word and you're thinking the futile thoughts of this world.

∼

The transformation of your thoughts leads to transformation in your words and actions as God's Word goes to work in you.

∼

Transformation isn't anger management. It's getting angry at your old management and having your new management formed in you.

∼

Consume God's Word not just to be informed but to be transformed.

∼

You've been given the mind of Christ and you're called to put it on so that you end up thinking like He does in everything.

∼

In Christ, you are called to simply trust that the One who created everything knows how it all works and that He'll teach you.

∼

If you believe that God's Word is true, then you must believe that what it says about you is true.

∼

Jesus lovingly, patiently teaches and transforms you; you can trust Him to disciple you and to demolish even the biggest strongholds.

∼

Not every thought that comes into your mind represents who you are.

*You are defined by the thoughts you choose and chew on,
not by all the ones that float through.*

~

*God is Father, Son, and Holy Spirit in loving, unified coexistence and
He created you to be one with the triune God and with each other.*

~

*Satan wants you imitating him, living in selfish codependency.
God wants you imitating Him, living in loving interdependence.*

~

*You were never meant to merely read and know God's Word;
He gave it to you so that you would become transformed by it.*

Transforming Prayer

Truth Number 7

Knowing what the Spirit taught about prayer through James, John, and Paul will help you pray through your transformation.

My Dream

I was riding on a futuristic transport that was being used to take us laborers to and from the job site. I knew in the dream that our work was a long way off and in a very dangerous and hostile environment. Sitting beside me was a worker who was much more senior than me. He was holding paperwork and information regarding our work and the workers. We began discussing a key worker who had died. I knew that the key worker was one of the pioneers of the work and one of the best and most knowledgeable at the job but, apparently, I didn't know the half of it. The man I talked with told me that this key worker had known more, by far, than any other; he knew every part of the job in every detail. In fact, it was his expertise that everyone, on every level, had always relied on.

The job we did was not only high-risk but high-profile, and this senior gentleman that I sat with now showed me a list of all the top television talk shows and news programs that had done shows on our work. When there was a controversy or problem at the job site, this key worker had been the one called on to answer people's concerns and questions. As I looked at the list, I saw that he had been on all of these shows many times, far more often than anyone else. The sad thing was, this senior worker explained, he was so good that everyone had merely relied on him instead of learning from him. Now there was no one who knew everything like he did and only a few who were experts at certain parts of the job. I could see his concern. Here we all were in a very important high-risk job that had an effect on the population of the world and all of us were merely doing what we were told to do without learning more from the one who really knew everything. The job, the equipment, and the job site would start falling apart with no one to help. Without this key worker we were all at risk and eventually everything would come to a screeching halt and perhaps a very bad ending.

We arrived at the shuttle terminal with heavy hearts. We knew that the replacement crew that waited to go out hadn't heard the sad news yet and out of respect we waited around to hear the announcement. The new workers saw our demeanor and sadness and wondered. They gathered to hear the announcement in silence. After the announcement, the new workers seemed unconcerned and unaffected. They just picked up their conversations as if nothing had happened, got on the shuttles en masse and went to work. I was dumbfounded! The new crew of workers hadn't known this key worker and seemed only concerned about doing their job and getting a paycheck. They didn't seem to care about the key worker and they certainly didn't have even a small portion of the commitment and care for the work, and how it affected all of us, like he had possessed. They had no understanding of the danger they were in or how much their indifference was going to impact the future.

To be continued...

In this section we'll look at the how your relationship with God and your prayer life wonderfully collates with your transformation. In order to do that we'll first need to establish some biblical basics about God's plan for your relationship with Him and your prayer life.

REALLY KNOWING GOD

It's always been God's plan to transform you into His image. Why? So that you could be His children, be one with Him, know and love Him and be known and loved by Him for all of eternity.

> "No longer will one teach his neighbor or his brother, saying, 'Know the LORD,' for they will all know Me, from the least to the greatest of them"—this is the LORD's declaration. "For I will forgive their wrongdoing and never again remember their sin" (Jeremiah 31:34).

God's focus in this verse is relationship. He said, "*they will all know me*" because He will forgive them. In other words, sin was merely the obstacle keeping them from His true desire, a relationship. Now that the obstacle has been removed, He wants to be known by His children. Jesus knew that He would lay down His life so the obstacle could be removed and you could know the Father like He did.

> Jesus told him, "I am the way, the truth, and the life. No one comes to the Father except through Me. If you know Me, you will also know My Father. From now on you do know Him and have seen Him" (John 14:6–7).

What Jeremiah put into the future, Jesus put into the present as He headed to the cross. Compare what both of them said: "*for they will all know Me*" and "*From now on you do know Him.*" Jesus knew that He was about to fulfill Jeremiah's prophecy. His task was all about restoring you to who you were created to be—God's children. He opened the way so you could "*come to the Father.*"

I love the words, "*from now on.*" Jesus knew that a relationship with the Father wasn't something that we'd earn but something that He'd gain for us. The day you received Jesus you were given the same relationship with the Father that Jesus had. You "*know Him*"—you just need to grow up into it as you're transformed.

> All things have been entrusted to Me by My Father. No one knows the Son except the Father, and no one knows the Father except the Son and anyone to whom the Son desires to reveal Him (Matthew 11:27).

When you know the Son, it's given to you to know the Father and Jesus desires to reveal Him to you! This revealing is not a one-time revealing for salvation or a brief glimpse of God. The word *reveal* here means to "take off the cover" or "disclose" so that something can be seen and known. Jesus opened the way for you to really know, experience, and walk with the Father.

> This is eternal life: that they may know You, the only true God, and the One You have sent—Jesus Christ (John 17:3).

Every part of us—the new creation—is wired and equipped for a deep, personal, and very real relationship with God (Father, Son, and Holy Spirit). Your heart calls out for it and when you sense God's presence or His touch you're filled with the fullness of joy.

> You make known to me the path of life; <u>in your presence there is fullness of joy</u>; at your right hand are pleasures forevermore (Psalm 16:11 ESV).

Your promised relationship and intimacy with God is the highest, most amazing thing that Jesus died to achieve for you. Just like everything else in your salvation, your relationship with God has a past, present, and future aspect. You were given an intimate relationship with Him (Father, Son, and Holy Spirit) the day you were saved, you are currently growing up into that relationship, and when you leave this planet that relationship will be taken to a whole new level—all by grace.

I remember a time when I felt like I just needed a hug from my Heavenly Father, and I went to Him with the image in my mind of me climbing up onto His lap. As I closed the door behind me and went to Him in prayer, He flashed a picture in my mind that edited the picture I had come with. The new picture was of Him reaching down, lovingly scooping me up and putting me on His lap, and He was happy I was there. I wept for some time, realizing anew how much He loves me and how much I can rely on His grace and promise to reveal Himself to me. He showed me that because of His love and grace, I didn't even have to climb up on His lap. He anticipated my coming and lovingly gathered me into His arms and drew me close to Himself. You already have an intimate loving relationship with the Father and there's no climbing necessary.

A child may look like their father but the key to really becoming like him is the child's relationship with him. Likewise the foundation for you being transformed into His image is your relationship with the Father, Son, and Holy Spirit. As you—by faith—grow up into these relationships you are transformed in them.

KNOWING HIS LOVE

When I learned God's promise through Moses' prophecy (Deuteronomy 30:6), that He would cause me to love Him with all my heart and soul, I trusted His promise, and my love for Him increased and took over. As my love for Him grew so did my desire to experience His love for me. Don't get me wrong, I knew through His Word that He loved me and I accepted that fact by faith. I wasn't trying to "feel" like He loved me or "feel" His love—our feelings can be misleading. There were even times I *experienced* His love for me—but I still somehow knew that there was more. Then one day while reading the Word, Jesus taught me something that changed me forever.

> I pray that you, being rooted and firmly established in love, <u>may be able to comprehend</u> with all the saints what is the length and width, height and depth of God's love, <u>and to know the Messiah's love that surpasses knowledge</u>, so you may be filled with all the fullness of God. <u>Now to Him who is able to do above and beyond all that we ask or think according to the power that works in us</u>— to Him be glory in the church and in Christ Jesus to all generations, forever and ever. Amen (Ephesians 3:17–21).

This amazing prayer that Paul prayed for the Ephesians is God's desire for every Christian. Let's look first at verse 20: "*Now to Him who is able to do above and beyond all that we ask or think according to the power that works in us…*" By ending his prayer this way Paul shows you that everything in the prayer is dependent on God's power at work within you and therefore will be done for you by His grace and power.

Now that you understand that, let's look at what Paul prayed about God's love for us. "*I pray that you, being rooted and firmly established in love, <u>may be able to comprehend</u> with all the saints what is the length and width, height and depth of God's love, and <u>to know the Messiah's love</u> that <u>surpasses knowledge</u>.*" Notice the conundrum: Paul prays that you would be able to "*comprehend*" and "*know*" something that "*surpasses knowledge.*" Looking at the original language, Paul asked God to help you perceive, understand, experience, and be sure of God's love which transcends and is beyond your ability to know and understand. How can you know something that's beyond knowing?

You cannot know God's love for you on your own because it's beyond your ability, but *"according to the power that works in us"* He reveals His love to you and takes your knowing and experience of His love beyond what you could, yourself, ask or think. And as Paul says in verse 21, God gets all of the glory because it's all a free gift in and through Christ Jesus.

The Apostle John wrote, *"God is love"* (1 John 4:8). Since God is love, you can't truly know Him without knowing His love; and Jesus can't truly reveal Him without revealing His love. There's a big difference between knowing that God loves you and knowing His love. He's given you the promise of knowing His love; you just need to receive it by grace through faith.

Since this truth from God's Word hit my heart and I started thanking God that I do know His love—renewing my mind with the truth—the knowledge of His love has been growing inside of me. It's not a feeling, it's a powerful knowing—a sense and assurance of His love—I just know He loves me *huge*. It's an indescribable gift that often brings me to tears of joy. Here's my point: the deeper I know His love the more I'm transformed by it.

He *really* loves you beyond what you can ask or think and He's ready to reveal His love to you, as you trust Him! Keep praying and trusting and never let this go! You are His child and you were made to know and be known by Him, to love Him and be loved by Him. It's who you are and it's all by grace. The more you grow in knowing how much He loves you the easier it is to trust Him, His promises, and His plan for you and that accelerates your transformation. Truly knowing that you're loved is an unshakeable foundation.

TRANSFORMED BY KNOWING HIM

God—Father, Son, and Holy Spirit—reveal themselves to you not only through the Word but also by walking with you and having you experience them according to His Word. As they do, Christ and the relationship He had with the Father is formed in you and that transforms you. Why? Because it's only in truly knowing God, not just about Him, that you can be transformed into His image.

In the Bible you see that the people who got really close to God (Enoch, Abraham, Moses, David) were all changed forever by Him. They were examples for us, pictures or samplings of what you have in Christ Jesus (Matthew 11:11). You are to become like Him by unwrapping the gift of knowing Him.

> And we all, with unveiled face, <u>beholding the glory of the Lord</u>, are being transformed into the same image from one degree of glory to another (2 Corinthians 3:18 ESV).

It's as you behold Him—yes, what the Word says about Him, but also Him—walking with Him, spending time with Him, talking with Him, and having Him reveal Himself and His love to you, that you're changed. I'm not talking about the supernatural encounters. Those are nice and Jesus had them but that's not what He relied on. I'm talking about growing daily by grace through faith in a deep realization of His presence with you and His love for you—knowing Him. God reveals who He is as He reveals Himself and you cannot help but be transformed as He does.

Let's look at a few important prayer fundamentals before looking specifically at praying through your transformation.

PRAYERS THAT DON'T WORK

As discussed previously, everything God has for you must be received by faith, because it's all given by His grace. That's so that everything God has promised you can be guaranteed (Romans 4:16; 5:1–2). If receiving anything from God depended on your works then it could never be guaranteed. Therefore, you should never pray prayers that are outside of your complete reliance on His grace. If you ever find yourself trying to talk God into answering your prayers about your transformation—or anything else—because you somehow deserve it, you really need it, or because you don't usually ask for much, etc., you've forgotten that it's all by grace through faith. Trying to convince God to be good because you deserve it is backwards. He is good and, in reality, you deserve nothing.

Also, the word "beg" should never be uttered in your prayers. A child who is confident in his father's love never needs to beg for anything. You must stop praying like you have to earn, beg for, or talk God into what

He's already promised you by grace. Strong, unshakable faith comes from knowing that God will do what He promised to do by grace and grace alone.

Prayer is about a relationship with God. You can count on God answering your prayers because He is good, you are in Christ, and you are loved immensely. In the same way, you're not transformed into His image because you deserve it, can talk God into it, and/or beg Him to do it. You're transformed because it's God's plan for you, Jesus paid for it, and you receive it by faith.

PRAYING GOD'S WILL

By now, I trust that you're convinced that transformation is God's will for you. However, you may still get caught up in wondering about the nuances of God's will: have I excluded myself, is the timing right, or what if God won't accomplish His will in my life for some unknown reason? After all, Jesus prayed, "If it be thy will", didn't He? No, He actually didn't use *those* words. But this idea can trip you up in your transformation. So let's look at what the Bible actually says about praying according to God's will. Jesus actually prayed:

> "Father, if You are willing, take this cup away from Me—nevertheless, not My will, but Yours, be done" (Luke 22:42).

Jesus is your example and He showed you by this prayer that it's okay for you to have a conversation with God about the things He calls you to, as long as you stay submitted. But Jesus was never in the dark about God's will. A very short time after Jesus prayed this prayer, He allowed Himself to be arrested, showing that He clearly knew the Father's will.

> At that, Jesus said to Peter, "Sheathe your sword! Am I not to drink the cup the Father has given Me?" (John 18:11).

Jesus' prayer doesn't demonstrate that you can't know God's will but that you *can*; Jesus knew God's will from the Word but in that moment He needed His Father's love, strength, and assurance so He asked for it, received it and acted accordingly; and then He immediately, willingly, and confidently started heading toward the cross. God's will for your life is your transformation into His image. On that foundation you can reach out to God and talk with Him about anything, knowing that He'll comfort, direct, and establish you in His will just like He did for Jesus.

Here's another verse that you need to understand about praying God's will:

> Now this is the confidence we have before Him: whenever we ask anything according to His will, He hears us. And if we know that He hears whatever we ask, we know that we have what we have asked Him for (1 John 5:14–15).

You may sometimes read these verses thinking that John posed a paradox. On one hand, you can have whatever you ask for. Wow! But on the other hand, if what you've asked for is somehow mysteriously not God's will, then you can't have it; so it seems you don't really get whatever you ask for. It's only a paradox if you think that you can't know God's will.

Why would John start out saying, "*Now this is the confidence we have before Him,*" if there's no way to know His will and therefore no way to know that you have what you've asked Him for? You saw earlier in James that if you don't pray in faith (assurance) you cannot "*receive anything from the Lord.*" Therefore, John must be assuming that you can know God's will and ask accordingly because that's the only way you can pray in faith and therefore receive.

Let's examine what John wrote a little closer. When do the different parts of the process that John mentions happen? It all happens in the context of your prayer session, when you're asking and He's hearing. The Message Bible clearly brings out the fact that knowing you've asked according to His will, that He's heard you, and that you have what you've asked for, all happen when you're praying.

> And how bold and free we then become in his presence, freely asking according to his will, sure that he's listening. And if we're confident that he's listening, we know that what we've asked for is as good as ours (1 John 5:14–15 MSG).

John is agreeing with what Jesus taught him:

> Therefore, I tell you, all the things you pray and ask for— believe that you have received them, and you will have them (Mark 11:24).

Jesus taught that you are to believe that you've received what you've prayed for when you pray—not when you see the answer and realize it was God's will, but when you pray. Again, that's the only way to pray in faith. John is teaching what the Master taught. You discover His will then you pray, and then you know by faith that you have what you've asked for.

Jesus and John agree: you can know God's will by getting into His Word and letting Jesus teach you and write it on your hearts. Once you know His will you can pray in full assurance of faith knowing that He hears you and that you have what we've asked for.

You have been predestined to be conformed to the image of His Son and you're to be transformed by the renewing of your mind until Christ is fully formed in you. There are no exceptions, there is nothing that can hold you back and the timing is now (2 Corinthians 6:2). God will transform you. He's promised it and declared it. He won't go back on His Word (Hebrews 6:17–18) and His Word will accomplish what He sent it to do. When you're praying about your transformation into Christ's image, you can know you're praying according to His will, that He hears you, and that you have what you're asking Him for. So you can trust Him and proceed like Abraham did.

> He did not waver in unbelief at God's promise but was strengthened in his faith and gave glory to God, because he was fully convinced that what he had promised He was also able to perform (Romans 4:20–21).

Now let's look specifically at how you are to pray through your transformation.

PRAYING THROUGH YOUR TRANSFORMATION

Prayer is all about relationship, knowing God, Father, Son, and Holy Spirit. You are transformed as you walk intimately with God, trusting Him to reveal Himself and His love. You *must* know that your transformation is His will, make it your hope, pray in faith (resisting doubt), and receive it through grace.

So how are you to pray through your transformation? The Holy Spirit taught you how when Paul wrote down how He prayed God's will for the churches. The prayers of Paul are focused on believers' growth in transformation. (Here's a list for you to look up: 1 Corinthians 1:4–9; Ephesians 1:15–19; 3:14–21; Philippians 1:3–6; 1:9–11; Colossians 1:9–14; 1 Thessalonians 5:23–24; 2 Thessalonians 1:11–12; 2:16–17; Philemon 1:6.)

Let's take a look at one of the most loved of Paul's prayers and learn. (Paul was quite consistent in how he prayed for believers so I'll use this one as an example and make reference to the rest.)

> This is why, since I heard about your faith in the Lord Jesus and your love for all the saints, I never stop giving thanks for you as I remember you in my prayers. I pray that the God of our Lord Jesus Christ, the glorious Father, would give you a spirit of wisdom and revelation in the knowledge of Him. I pray that the perception of your mind may be enlightened so you may know what is the hope of His calling, what are the glorious riches of His inheritance among the saints, and what is the immeasurable greatness of His power to us who believe, according to the working of His vast strength (Ephesians 1:15–19).

Paul prayed that God would take you beyond mere knowledge and cause you to understand everything that Jesus bought for you, and cause you to really "get it" so that your mind is renewed. He wanted God to do that in you so that you'd know and experience what you're called to (being transformed into Christ's image); everything that is yours in Christ Jesus (His love, your inheritance, the Kingdom, God's promises, etc.); and God's power working in you (which He provides in order to make all of that a reality). Or very simply put: Paul wanted God to cause you to really know and understand the Gospel so that you could be transformed into who you are in Christ and receive and live in all you've been given in Christ. You receive all this by knowing and relying on His great power that's at work within you.

Jesus exemplified what Paul prayed for us. He knew who He was, what was His, and the power of the Father that worked so mightily in and through Him. All of Paul's prayers were about you following in Jesus' footsteps and being transformed into His image. So by looking at both the content and approach of Paul's prayers, you can learn something about how to pray.

The first thing to notice is that Paul prayed in an attitude of thanksgiving (1 Corinthians 1:4; Ephesians 1:16; Philippians 1:3; Colossians 1:12). He thanked God for those he prayed for and also for what Jesus had accomplished for them. Jesus' work is done. You already are a new creation—created in His image—so you thank Him for what He's already accomplished and for working in you as He promised. The evidence of faith is thankfulness. Your transformation prayers should be bathed in thanksgiving. Even when you're not feeling thankful, choosing to be thankful will get you back in His strength more quickly.

Next, everything Paul prayed was God's will according to the Gospel. Paul prayed God's will so that he could know that he was heard and could stand in faith. You follow his example by praying what you know God's Word says regarding your transformation.

I memorize (not necessarily word for word) what the Bible says about God's will for me in certain areas and make a personalized topical verse-montage that I pray when needed. What is a topical verse-montage, you ask? It's just a compilation of the Bible verses that I've put in my heart for each topic I pray about.

When I'm affirming what He's promised about me knowing Him, I pray a topical verse-montage something like this: "Thank You Father that according to Your promises in Christ Jesus I know You and Your love. My fellowship is with You, Your Son, and the Holy Spirit. Jesus, I'm one of Your sheep, so I thank You that I know You and You know me like You knew the Father, and He knew You when You walked this earth. I hear Your voice and the voice of a stranger I will not follow. I thank You, Jesus, that You call me Your friend, manifest Yourself to me and reveal the Father to me. Please continue to work within me and cause me to grow in this amazing relationship that You've given me by grace." That's my "topical verse-montage" for knowing Him.

As you meditate on different verses about your transformation and pray about them—whether it's about your relationship with Him, growing in the fruit of the Spirit, being free from sin, doing the works that Jesus did, or any other transformation topic—you'll develop your own personal verse-montage prayers. I don't have the "knowing Him" verse-montage prayer above memorized and I don't repeat it into the air like it's magic. I pray it, talking to God in a conversational way. I think about it, praise Him for it, stop and talk to Him about what the verses promise and mean to me, and I listen to and learn from Him.

The next thing to notice about Paul's prayers is that he consistently prayed that believers—the church—would know and deeply understand what Jesus accomplished for them (Ephesians 1:17–18; 3;18–19; Philippians 1:9, 10; Colossians 1:9–10; Philemon 1:6). You should never think that you know all of what God has for you and wants to do in you. Paul prayed, *"Now to Him who is able to do above and beyond all that we ask or think according to the power that works in us"* (Ephesians 3:20). You should pray that He increases your knowledge of Him and causes you to truly understand, so that He can do more in and through you than you can ask or think.

What Paul prayed for each church varied depending on what they were learning and going through. This demonstrates that your verse-montage prayers should be topical and appropriate to what God is teaching you. Also, since God is continually expanding your transformation, you should continually be adding new verse-montage prayers to your repertoire, and new verses to the ones you are currently praying.

Next you see that Paul always prayed on the foundation of grace—asking for strength and encouragement and for a revelation of God's great power that was at work within to transform him (1 Corinthians 1:4, 8; Ephesians 1:19; 3:16, 20–21; Philippians 1:6; Colossians 1:11; 1 Thessalonians 5:23; 2 Thessalonians 1:12; Philemon 1:6). Every verse-montage prayer should contain something like this: "Thank You for working this within me, Lord, by Your grace, promises, and power. I give You all the glory for my amazing transformation."

Also, Paul said he never stopped praying these prayers (Ephesians 1:16; 1 Corinthians 1:4; Philippians 1:4; Colossians 1:9; 2 Thessalonians 1:11). You should pray your topical verse-montage prayers when you need His grace in the moment (Hebrews 4:16), but you should also follow Paul's example, and pray transforming prayers constantly.

The Holy Spirit taught Paul how to pray to the Father continually (1 Thessalonians 5:17), thank Him and praise Him, stay focused on Jesus his Master and Teacher, fellowship with the Holy Spirit, defeat the enemy, put off and put on, cast down strongholds, renew his mind, build his faith, and powerfully fuel his transformation into Christ's image, all at the same time. He did it by continuously praying God's will and Word.

When God started encouraging me in this spiritual exercise, I realized how unintentional I was in my thinking. I began to trust the Holy Spirit to help me stop my mind from wandering aimlessly and get it on His Word. Jesus promises that the Holy Spirit will remind us of the things He's taught us (John 14:26), and does He ever! It was awkward at first, but as I trusted Him to help me, the scriptures would start rolling off my tongue. Try it! The exercise will encourage and energize you; the Holy Spirit will fill you up and the Lord will start teaching you, and as He does, more verses will come. Then stop and ponder and talk to Him and rejoice over the truth.

The more you pray this way the more your personal verse-montage prayers just become a springboard into God's river and the easier it gets to dive in. Whether you're putting off and putting on by praying the Word and renewing your mind in the midst of life, or you're sitting down for a long time of fellowship with Him, the more you practice the more it flows.

Please remember, it's a relationship. You may start out memorizing verses and quoting them mechanically to God but don't stay there. Ask Him to work in you and stop after quoting a few verses to thank Him, praise Him, or just talk to Him about what His Word says. Ask the Holy Spirit to guide you and remind you of what you've been taught, and ask the Lord to teach you. You may have to start by writing out the verses for each topical verse-montage prayer and reading them in prayer, and that's okay. As you read them and stay focused on Him they'll make their home inside you. You may even want to keep a file where you write out verses by topic.

You might be asking at this point, "Shouldn't I just pray from my heart in my own words?" Yes, you should always pray from your heart and you should often use your own words. The problem is that you've probably wasted too much time already praying your own words and your own agenda and getting nowhere. If you trust Him and you've truly made Jesus Lord and His image your goal, then you need to stay focused on His agenda—and His Word is His agenda. So you should pray God's words *and* your words from your heart, but you should always let His words be the guide for yours.

And finally, Paul undoubtedly prayed similar prayers for himself, but in the Word he prayed them for others. When you're praying for others use the same model, letting His words guide yours. Also remember: no matter what you're praying about for others, follow Paul's lead and pray for them in the context of transformation; your prayer goal for others is to see them walking in who God has already created them to be.

My dream continued…

I told you about a dream God gave me about a futuristic, high-risk job that impacted the whole world. In the dream, a worker, very much my senior, discussed with me the loss of the most important worker. He was the only one who had known everything. Everyone had relied on Him and His knowledge and He had kept everyone safe and working. Without Him you were all at risk and the enterprise seemed doomed. When the younger, newer workers were told, however, they were unaffected. They only seemed concerned with getting to work, doing their job, and getting a paycheck. In the dream I was amazed at the workers' disconnect with the gravity of the situation.

The workers represented those of us who are born into God's Kingdom. The high-risk, important-to-the-whole-planet job is spreading the Gospel, and seeing people transferred from the domain of darkness into God's Kingdom. The shuttle represented us *"going into all the world"* with the Gospel. The senior worker who explained the problem to me represented the Holy Spirit. The senior worker that he discussed with me represented Jesus, the Head of His Body, the Church.

Just before Jesus ascended back to the Father, He told us to *"remember and pay close attention"* to the fact that He'd always be with us. The early church remembered and they became His coworkers in spreading the Gospel.

> And they went out and preached everywhere, the Lord working with them and confirming the word by the accompanying signs (Mark 16:20).

As Jesus' disciple, you are to walk with Him, learn from Him, learn to walk as He walked, and become just like Him. The central focus of

Jesus' life is summed up in a few simple things that He said repeatedly: He knew the Father, He was one with the Father, He only did and said what He saw and heard the Father doing and saying, and He walked in the anointing and power of the Holy Spirit. Before He left, He said this:

> "Peace to you! <u>As the Father has sent Me, I also send you</u>" (John 20:21).

You are, first and foremost, a child of God, a disciple of Jesus Christ, and the temple of the Holy Spirit. You are blessed to be called into intimate fellowship with all three members of the Godhead by grace. It's not only your greatest privilege and blessing, but your greatest asset for transformation and accomplishing the great commission. Yet, because many believers haven't understood that this great privilege is a gift that they can walk in by grace through faith, prayer for many has become a struggle.

Jesus is the Head of the Body and in this dream He showed me that many who are His, and who work in His Kingdom, have become severed from the Head. To be transformed and to powerfully impact this world you need a real, intimate, and powerful relationship. Run to Him and start growing in relationship with Him by His grace and promises. There is no greater joy than to receive the greatest gift ever offered—oneness and intimacy with the Father, Son, and Spirit.

It's time to look at what Jesus was specifically telling believers to do when He said to go make disciples. But first I'd like to talk with you briefly about how to "rest and run" in your transformation.

POWER POINTS FROM TRUTH NUMBER 7
Quotes for Sharing on Social Media

Jesus knew that a relationship with the Father wasn't something that we'd earn but something that He'd gain for us.

∽

Every part of us—the new creation—is wired and equipped for a deep, personal, and very real relationship with God.

∽

Your promised relationship and intimacy with God is the highest, most amazing thing that Jesus died to achieve for you.

∽

He reveals His love to you and takes your knowing and experience of His love beyond what you could, yourself, ask or think.

∽

Since God is love, you can't truly know Him without knowing His love.

∽

There's a big difference between knowing that God loves you and knowing His love.

∽

You are His child and you were made to know and be known by Him, to love Him and be loved by Him.

∽

Truly knowing that you're loved is an unshakeable foundation.

*It's only in truly knowing God, not just about Him,
that you can be transformed into His image.*

∼

*God reveals who He is as He reveals Himself and you
cannot help but be transformed as He does.*

∼

*You should never pray prayers that are outside of
your complete reliance on His grace.*

∼

*Trying to convince God to be good because you deserve it is backwards.
He is good and, in reality, you deserve nothing.*

∼

*You must stop praying like you have to earn, beg for, or
talk God into what He's already promised you by grace.*

∼

*Unshakable faith comes from knowing that God will do
what He promised to do by grace and grace alone.*

∼

*You're transformed because it's God's plan for you,
Jesus paid for it, and you receive it by faith.*

∼

*Once you know His will you can pray in full assurance of faith
knowing that He hears you and that you have what we've asked for.*

∼

*When you're praying about your transformation into Christ's
image, you can know you're praying according to His will.*

*Know that your transformation is His will, make it your hope,
pray in faith (resisting doubt), and receive it through grace.*

∼

The prayers of Paul are focused on believers' growth in transformation.

∼

*All of Paul's prayers were about you following in Jesus' footsteps
and being transformed into His image.*

∼

The evidence of faith is thankfulness.

∼

*You should pray God's words and your words from your heart,
but you should always let His words be the guide for yours.*

∼

*A prayer goal for others is to see them walking
in who God has already created them to be.*

∼

*As Jesus' disciple, you are to walk with Him, learn from Him,
learn to walk as He walked, and become just like Him.*

∼

*You are, first and foremost, a child of God, a disciple of
Jesus Christ, and the temple of the Holy Spirit.*

∼

*There is no greater joy than to receive the greatest gift ever offered—
oneness and intimacy with the Father, Son, and Spirit.*

Conclusion

Making Disciples

Getting back on track with the Great Commission

My Dream...

I was taken to this older but beautifully built apartment building. The inside was very unique. The apartments all faced a covered atrium-like common area. From inside you could see all of the railed walkways and stairs that led to each level and to each apartment. There were places to walk, sit, play, and gather in the common area. Although I was being shown around, I felt like I belonged. I was somehow part of the community. It was mealtime and my guide told me that things worked differently here. As I watched, people started opening up their doors and windows to the common area. Some apartments had large doors and windows; others appeared to have sliding walls so that they could completely open their living quarters. Within minutes, it seemed like the whole building was one big open community.

Each apartment was unique and every one had a table laden with wonderful food. The families were from every ethnic background and tradition so the food on every table was quite different. I understood right away that at mealtimes everyone prepared food and shared it with everyone else in the apartment building. Everyone grabbed a plate and walked around talking, visiting, tasting, and helping themselves to whatever food they wanted. Then everyone sat in different areas, visiting and enjoying the food and company. It was an amazing community experience and I remember thinking that it was a great idea!

As I walked around meeting people, I found this small door in a more obscure part of the building. I couldn't see inside because the apartment wasn't very open. I made my way in and found a lone man in a small room sitting behind a desk. His only food was in a small plastic leftover container and he was eating from it himself, as he offered me some. My attention was drawn to a Bible that sat on his desk and I started up a conversation with the man about it. He responded by saying something about studying. I got excited. I told him that I loved to study God's Word and asked him what he was studying. He had barely looked up at me but had continued to work on whatever he was working on. He reached over briefly and opened his Bible to the front, tapped on a page, and said, "Just this part."

I looked at what he had tapped on and turned a few pages. It appeared that he only read and studied the notes or catechism that was in the front of his Bible and not the Bible itself. In the final scene I was down in the common area again enjoying great food with everyone who was crowded around visiting and enjoying themselves.

To be continued…

REST AND RUN

Put together, the words "Rest and Run" sound like a contradiction, but when it comes to the topic of growing in grace, these two words must work together.

> "<u>Come to Me, all of you who are weary and burdened, and I will give you rest</u>. All of you, <u>take up My yoke</u> and <u>learn from Me</u>, because I am gentle and humble in heart, <u>and you will find rest for yourselves</u>. For My yoke is easy and My burden is light" (Matthew 11:28–30).

Knowing that Jesus has already accomplished your complete salvation, you do your "*easy*" and "*light*" part: you go to Him, take up His yoke and learn from Him, trusting Him to teach and transform you. You run *to* Him and then *with* Him towards the hope of your calling, resting in His complete work and His grace. Paul talked about "running the race", and he ran it full tilt because he knew how to run in God's grace (1 Corinthians 15:10).

Paul believed that his growth and work were empowered by God's grace and his faith was demonstrated by what he did by grace. All of your prayers, actions, and efforts cannot get you transformed, but when you respond in obedience to Him because you know He is at work within you, then your efforts demonstrate your faith. When God sees your faith He empowers you to keep moving.

If you remain where you are, doing what you've always done, you'll continue to get the same results. If this book has merely been informing you and you haven't yet begun to cry out, respond, and act, please stop now and talk to the Father. God's grace was "*not ineffective*" in Paul because he believed and started running. God's grace becomes effective in you when you mix in your faith and begin moving.

God has given you everything you need for transformation and the core of that provision is your relationship with Him—Father, Son, and Holy Spirit. Your transformation is built on that foundation and therefore the whole process is relational. Because of God's love for you He acts according to His grace. Because of your love for Him you act according to your faith. You respond to Him now, consistently, and forever, turning to Him, talking to Him about everything, and trusting Him; and He continues to speak to you, teach you, and transform you according to His promise. As you move with Jesus in relationship and obedience it's God's love, grace, and power that moves you.

He calls you to "rest and run"—to trust in His love and grace and run in faith. Resting in Him doesn't mean you ever stop responding and growing, and running in Him doesn't mean you ever stop resting and trusting in His complete work. Your faith in His complete work should catapult you forward. Even when you struggle and don't feel like transformation is happening, keep moving forward anyway, praying His Word and turning to Him for strength, encouragement, and faith. He provides it.

Samson walked out to face a huge army with nothing available to use as a weapon but a donkey's jawbone. When he went out, God's power hit him and that army was no match. David ran at Goliath armed with only a slingshot, trusting God to give him the victory. When you run because you know what He's promised to do in you, demonstrate your faith and you receive more of God's grace.

While I was writing this book, God gave me a powerful picture that still brings tears to my eyes. I saw a field full of wounded soldiers lying all over the ground suffering and dying. Then I saw them begin to stand on their feet, and as they did they recovered from their wounds and stood strong for battle again. I knew that these were Christians of all descriptions who, at one point, felt called to make a difference but who had been burnt out, discouraged, hurt, knocked down, and broken. As I saw these people, I was overwhelmed by the compassion God felt for them. Then the Father showed me that this message of complete transformation by grace through faith would help a great number of those wounded soldiers to rise up into mighty warriors for the Kingdom—more powerful and effective, and having a greater impact, than they had ever thought possible.

If you feel like this picture applies to you, stop and pray right now. The Lord loves you! And by His grace He will heal you, restore you, transform your life, and use you to bring His grace to others.

What would happen if the whole Body of Christ started walking with the Master in the transformation He's called us to? I believe it would bless the nations and change our planet. I believe that's always been God's plan.

A VISION FOR MAKING DISCIPLES

Now, I'd like to examine what the Bible says about how the early church "made disciples" and encourage you to not only continue in your own transformation, but also to reach out and help make disciples so others can be transformed. To make disciples for Jesus you can't stop at getting someone converted. You need to show people how to walk with Him, be taught by Him, and become just like Him—to be transformed into His image.

To be clear, you become a disciple when you become a new creation; but you need to be taught how to actually be, and to walk as, a disciple. Becoming a disciple and never learning how to be one is like enrolling in law school and calling yourself a lawyer but never attending classes. The early church understood that the goal was transformation and the way to get there was to learn to walk with Jesus.

When I entered the Kingdom, I was a disciple ready to be trained: my life was surrendered and I had tons of zeal, but unfortunately, I was not shown how to be and walk as a disciple of Christ Jesus. I'm absolutely rejoicing in what God is doing in me and I'm not regretting the past, but for the sake of learning and contributing to the growth of the Church, I'm compelled to ask: where would I be today had I been taught how to walk as His disciple thirty-five years ago? More importantly, where would the Church be today if everyone who entered the Church in the past thirty-five years had been made into a mature disciple of the Lord Jesus?

The goal of the early New Testament Church was to make disciples for Jesus and they turned the world upside down. Here are just a few verses where Paul, by the Spirit, stated his vision for the churches he was involved with.

> We proclaim Him, warning and <u>teaching everyone</u> with all wisdom, <u>so that we may present everyone mature in Christ. I labor for this, striving with His strength that works powerfully in me</u> (Colossians 1:28–29).
>
> My children, I am again suffering labor pains for you <u>until Christ is formed in you</u> (Galatians 4:19).
>
> Therefore, <u>be imitators of God</u>, as dearly loved children (Ephesians 5:1).
>
> And <u>we all</u>, with unveiled face, beholding the glory of the Lord, <u>are being transformed into the same image from one degree of glory to another</u> (2 Corinthians 3:18 ESV).

Paul's expressed goal for each member of each church was that they become mature in Christ, imitators of God, so that Christ would be fully formed in them and they'd be transformed into His image. Paul's objective was the Great Commission; he was *"making disciples"* of Jesus, and a disciple is to become—in all respects—exactly like the Master (Matthew 10:25). This objective was so clear that Paul stated that if the churches he started weren't filled with men and women who were just like Jesus, all his work would have been for nothing.

> Do all things without grumbling or disputing, that <u>you may be blameless and innocent, children of God without blemish</u> in the midst of a crooked and twisted generation, *among whom you shine as lights in the world*, <u>holding fast to the word of life</u>, so that in the day of Christ I may be proud <u>that I did not run in vain or labor in vain</u> (Philippians 2:14–16 ESV).

The clear vision for the churches that Paul ministered to was that each member would become Christlike (blameless, innocent, and without blemish), walk in relationship with God (children of God), do Christ's work (shine as lights in this world), and know the Word so they could be renewed and transformed by it (holding fast to the word of life). If Paul's results were short of that goal he felt that his labor would have been in vain. Why are we content with less?

Today, if you asked people who attend church on a regular basis why they come to church you would be glad to hear something like this: "To be intentionally taught by my spiritual leaders how to be a disciple of Christ Jesus—knowing, loving, being taught by and following Him—so that I can be transformed into His image, become all God created me to be, and become fully equipped to impact the world and expand God's Kingdom with my life and gifts; all in partnership with my brothers and sisters in Christ."

More often, however, the answers you hear are: "For fellowship." "To worship God." "Obedience to God." "For spiritual growth." "So I can be a better person." These are all common answers but they all fall far short of God's purpose for the Body. Jesus said, *"I wish that you were cold or hot"* (Revelation 3:15). We need to be careful not to set up churches to facilitate the lukewarm.

Jesus was your example and although He regularly attended synagogue, He went out from there to share the love of the Father. Then He made disciples and sent them out to do the same. And finally He told His Disciples to go and make disciples of all nations so that those disciples could do the same. The local church is to be a boot-camp where new believers are made into Jesus' disciples and then sent out to live as He did.

> And He personally gave some to be apostles, some prophets, some evangelists, some pastors and teachers, <u>for the training of the saints in the work of ministry, to build up the body of Christ</u>, until <u>we all</u> reach unity in the faith and in the knowledge of God's Son, <u>growing into a mature man with a stature measured by Christ's fullness</u> (Ephesians 4:11–13).

Those in the Body are to do the *"work of ministry"* and the primary task of the ministers/spiritual leaders in the church is to be the boot-camp instructors. They are called to make disciples for Jesus, not only teaching them *"the words of Christ"* and *"the apostles' doctrine,"* but showing them how to be discipled from the inside-out and helping them to be transformed into Christ's image so they can go out into the world with the love of the Father.

Jesus said He'd build His Church and He told us to make disciples. When you attempt to do His part and ignore yours, you fail. When you get your part right you'll see Him build His Church. Why? Because His plan has always been to build His Church by having His disciples make disciples. That works because when you're connected to the Head and following Him He can use you, as He wills, to build His Church.

TWO PHASES OF DISCIPLESHIP

Biblically, the process of discipleship seems to have two phases. The first phase establishes the new believer in the Gospel and shows them how to walk with, follow, and be taught and transformed by Jesus. In the second phase believers walk out their transformation to maturity with Jesus, in the company of believers, who are all doing the same.

When Paul established and/or helped establish a new community of believers, his stated first goal was to see Christ formed in them. In this verse Paul let the Galatians know that because they were listening to error that he might have to restart the process.

> My children, I am <u>again</u> suffering labor pains for you until <u>Christ is formed in you</u> (Galatians 4:19).

The word "again" shows that Paul's original purpose in spending time with the church in Galatia and teaching them was to have Christ formed in them. The fact that Paul used the metaphor of childbirth and labor pains shows that he didn't believe that the new birth process—in regards to *his* part in that process—was finished just because they now believed. Paul knew His responsibility was to make disciples for Jesus, not just converts, so his *"labor pains"* were not over until those he brought to faith had Christ fully formed in them. This meant that Paul taught and trained them until they knew how to recognize, learn from, follow and be transformed by the Master from the inside-out (Galatians 2:20–21; Colossians 1:27).

This discipleship process didn't start with Paul. On the day of Pentecost the church grew by 3,000 people and it kept growing. Those new converts knew little or nothing about Jesus and His teachings and even less about having Christ in them discipling and transforming them. The Disciples—that is, the twelve Apostles—were charged with making these new converts into active disciples of Jesus and they made sure that they kept focused on that.

> So those who accepted his message were baptized, and that day about 3,000 people were added to them. <u>And they devoted themselves to the apostles' teaching</u>, to fellowship, to the breaking of bread, and to prayers (Acts 2:41–42).

The first thing that new converts were taught was that they needed to be "*devoted... to the apostles' teaching*"—that they needed to be taught by the Apostles until they knew how to be disciples of Jesus. The concept of "get born again and get a little Christian teaching when you can" was not on the menu. When someone came into the Kingdom, they were taken aside and made into a disciple of the King. A few years later you see the early church making church structure and growth decisions without compromising their original commission.

> So the Twelve called a meeting of the disciples. They said, "<u>It wouldn't be right for us to abandon our responsibilities for preaching and teaching the Word of God</u> to help with the care of the poor. So, friends, choose seven men from among you whom everyone trusts, men full of the Holy Spirit and good sense, and we'll assign them this task" (Acts 6:2–3 MSG).

The Twelve spent *all* of their time preaching to the lost and teaching the new converts. They knew they needed to teach the new converts until they knew how to walk as His disciples and they spent every waking hour doing exactly that. The result? The above appointment of deacons happened somewhere between two and three years after the initial outpouring of the Holy Spirit. So the deacons that were chosen would have been less than three years old in Christ at that point. Yet, Stephen was said to be full of the Holy Spirit, full of faith and wisdom, and full of power and grace (Acts 6:3, 5, 8). The scripture also says that he performed *"great wonders and signs among the people"* and that those who opposed him *"were unable to stand up against his wisdom and the Spirit by whom he was speaking"* (vs. 8–10).

Today, a person with that resume would be the keynote speaker in the largest Christian conferences. Yet Stephen was a relatively new Christian who had just been promoted to being a deacon. How was this possible? When he became a Christian he began to sit under the Disciples' teaching and he kept being taught and kept learning until Christ was fully formed in him—until he knew how to learn from, be transformed by, be directed by, and work with the Master. All this was accomplished because the Apostles refused to get distracted from their task of making disciples for Jesus.

And Stephen wasn't an anomaly. Another one of the seven deacons, Philip, did astounding things for the Lord as well (Acts 8:4–40). There were also many other disciples spreading the Gospel and doing exploits by God's Spirit at this point (Acts 11:19–21), probably including the other five deacons. The stories of Stephen and Philip were likely recorded as highlights because of Stephen's martyrdom and the fact that Philip brought the Gospel to the Samaritans. If Luke had written about everyone and everything that was happening, the book of Acts would have been huge. In the early church, Stephen and Philip were just regular Christians who were taught how to be Jesus' disciples.

Look at the qualifications for those original deacons:

> Therefore, brothers, select from among you seven men of good reputation, full of the Spirit and wisdom, whom we can appoint to this duty (Acts 6:3).

All seven chosen were new Christians (by modern standards) yet they were known for their strong Christian character, for being full of the Holy Spirit, and for the wisdom of God that flowed out of them. Why? Because they were taught how to be disciples of Christ Jesus (1 Corinthians 1:30).

The early church worked and grew by this model. The mature disciples spent much focused time making disciples by teaching the new converts until Christ was formed in them. This cannot be accomplished with one sermon and a home group once a week. The exact details of the system they used are not recorded, but we know that teachers taught the new converts constantly in a focused, deliberate way. Both the church leaders and the converts knew that the goal was to reproduce Christ in each Christian. That was the communicated and shared vision from the start.

Let's look at what we do know about this process from scripture.

> Every day in the temple complex, and in various homes, they continued teaching and proclaiming the good news that Jesus is the Messiah (Acts 5:42).

The Disciples taught nonstop in public places and in homes. The Apostles' goal was to preach the Gospel of conversion to the unconverted and the Gospel of transformation to the converted, until all were walking as His disciples. Let's look at what happened when a church started in Antioch:

> Then the report about them was heard by the church that was at Jerusalem, and they sent out Barnabas to travel as far as Antioch. When he arrived and saw the grace of God, he was glad, and he encouraged all of them to remain true to the Lord with a firm resolve of the heart, for he was a good man, full of the Holy Spirit and of faith. And large numbers of people were added to the Lord. Then he went to Tarsus to search for Saul, and when he found him he brought him to Antioch. For a whole year they met with the church and taught large numbers. The disciples were first called Christians in Antioch (Acts 11:22–26).

When the leaders in Jerusalem heard about the converts in Antioch, what was their first thought? To establish them as disciples of Christ by teaching and training them. Barnabas was sent and he secured the help of Saul (Paul) to get the job done. Paul and Barnabas spent a whole year there teaching the *"large numbers"* of converts how to be His disciples. You need to be careful not to read these verses with your one-sermon-and-a-home-group-a-week mindset. When Paul taught, it was often by his own description, *"night and day"* (Acts 20:31). Paul and Barnabas taught and trained the converts and the converts listened and learned until Christ was formed in them.

Paul did the same thing in Ephesus:

> Then he entered the synagogue and spoke boldly over a period of three months, engaging in discussion and trying to persuade them about the things of the kingdom of God. But when some became hardened... he withdrew from them and met separately with the disciples, conducting discussions <u>every day</u> in the lecture hall of Tyrannus. And this went on for <u>two years, so that all the inhabitants of Asia, both Jews and Greeks, heard the message about the Lord</u> (Acts 19:8–10).

Although the Bible doesn't specify, tradition says that Paul probably taught from 11:00 AM to 4:00 PM (during the hottest part of the day) every day in the hall of Tyrannus. Paul made teaching the Word to new converts his priority (Acts 20:27, 31–32). Paul concentrated on making disciples of Jesus and ended up impacting most of the Roman province of Asia (Acts 19:10, 26) as Jesus built His church.

There are many more verses that confirm that the early church converts were taught intentionally and intensively:

> Now I urge you, brothers, to watch out for those who cause dissensions and obstacles <u>contrary to the doctrine you have learned</u>. Avoid them... (Romans 16:17).

> Therefore as you have received Christ Jesus the Lord, <u>walk in Him</u>, rooted and built up in Him and established in the faith, <u>just as you were taught</u>... (Colossians 2:6–7; see also 1:5–7).

> Until I come, give your attention to <u>public reading, exhortation, and teaching</u> (1 Timothy 4:13).

> ...<u>holding to</u> the <u>faithful message as taught</u>, so that he will be able both to encourage with sound teaching and to refute those who contradict it (Titus 1:9).

The converts in the early church were taught and made into Jesus' disciples right away and from there encouraged to *"walk in Him," "holding to"* what they were taught. The writer of Hebrews states:

> Although by this time you ought to be teachers, you need someone to teach you the basic principles of God's revelation again. You need milk, not solid food. Now everyone who lives on milk is inexperienced with the message about righteousness, because he is an infant (Hebrews 5:12–13).

Notice the word *"again."* The New Testament writers assumed that everyone had been taught and made into disciples of Jesus according to the Great Commission. It was also assumed that everyone could grow to the place where they could teach so that making disciples through intentional and progressive teaching and training wouldn't stop.

Paul was confident that the church at Rome had the teaching-and-making-disciples program working well. He wrote:

> My brothers, I myself am convinced about you that you also are full of goodness, filled with all knowledge, and able to instruct one another (Romans 15:14).

Paul wanted the churches to not only make disciples but to also continually raise up teachers who could do the same.

> And what you have heard from me in the presence of many witnesses, commit to faithful men who will be able to teach others also (2 Timothy 2:2).

So the first phase of discipleship was to make disciples by teaching and training new converts how to be Jesus' disciples—until Christ was fully formed in them. This first phase was intentional, progressive, intense, and never optional.

The second phase of discipleship happens when the newly-trained disciple—who is now following, learning, and being transformed by Jesus—is released into the Body of Christ and begins to grow further alongside the other disciples in life and ministry. Read Ephesians 4:11–16. There, Paul teaches that the ministers in the church are to be involved in *"training of the saints in the work of ministry"* (vs. 12), and take responsibility to see that the whole body comes to maturity. However, he goes on to explain that *"the whole body, fitted and knit together by every supporting ligament, promotes the growth of the body for building up itself in love by the proper working of each individual part"* (vs. 16). So the leaders of the church are to teach phase one and oversee phase two, as it's done in the body by the body, ensuring that all come to maturity in Christ.

We have often tried skipping phase one, placing new converts into the body, naively hoping that they will develop an intimate relationship with Jesus and grow to maturity by osmosis. This of course doesn't work because the intentional, progressive, and intense birth process of delivering, establishing, and feeding the new Christian until they are connected to Christ doesn't happen. Therefore, we fill our churches with people who often aren't much different than they were when they were first saved, and who are not growing in Christ. Then we wonder why our churches don't grow, or grow without growing up. The only way every part of His Body can help mature the Body is if all of them have first been made into disciples of Jesus, so they're all connected to the Head.

Imagine what the church would look like if every current member and every new member was taught and trained to be a real disciple of Jesus! What if our churches were full of people like the first seven deacons; true disciples of Jesus, full of His Spirit and wisdom? Imagine and pray.

HOW NOT TO MAKE DISCIPLES

I would like your understanding and grace for a few minutes while I talk frankly about discipleship and some misconceptions we've had about it. Please understand that I'm not criticizing anyone or anyone else's efforts. I merely want to be sure that you understand biblically what discipleship is so that we can move forward from where we are.

First, discipleship is not only for new believers; you never stop being His disciples and He never stops teaching and transforming you. The Apostle Paul understood this and didn't think that he had "arrived."

> <u>Not that I have already reached the goal or am already fully mature</u>, but I make every effort to take hold of it because I also have been taken hold of by Christ Jesus. Brothers, I do not consider myself to have taken hold of it. <u>But one thing</u>

<u>I do: Forgetting what is behind and reaching forward to what is ahead</u>, I pursue as my goal the prize promised by God's heavenly call in Christ Jesus. Therefore, <u>all who are mature should think this way</u> (Philippians 3:12–15).

Notice that Paul wanted those who were already mature to think like him and continue pressing forward in their transformation. The early church taught new converts how to be Jesus' disciples so that they could go on to maturity by being discipled by the Master. In the second phase the new believers continued to grow as His disciples in the Body.

I've been a Christian for more than three decades and been in the ministry for twenty-five years and by normal standards have been very successful in it. Yet, I'm more excited now about walking with my Lord, learning from Him, and moving to the next level than I've ever been. Discipleship doesn't stop. It just keeps getting better.

Next, discipleship isn't merely attending a "New Believers" class and learning basic doctrines. That is definitely part of the process but that alone will not make you a real, active disciple of Jesus. A new disciple must be taught how to be with, walk with, and fellowship with Jesus 24/7. They must be taught how to hear from, learn from, and be transformed by Him through the indwelling of the Holy Spirit. Their walk with Jesus, being discipled from the inside-out by Him, is to be as real as the discipleship the Twelve experienced. But remember, Jesus told them that what was coming was better (John 16:7). It's essential to teach the Word but unless a Christian knows how to be taught and transformed by Jesus they will merely be informed instead of transformed.

Also, any kind of discipleship that focuses on cleaning up the outside of the person, hoping the inside will follow, will not work. Teaching that to be a disciple you must finish certain courses, practice certain disciplines, complete certain tasks, and develop certain habits is works. I'm not saying that all of those things are unimportant; I am saying, however, that anything short of teaching and training a new convert how to truly know, walk with, learn from, and become like Jesus—by grace alone—is not making disciples.

Another concept that won't work is "patchwork discipleship." This is the idea that if you have enough church programs and sermons on every topic for every shape, description, and age of Christian and make them all available, somehow everyone will get what they need. Although most church programs are well intentioned and helpful, even a well-placed abundance of them will not replace the first phase of making disciples. No teacher, preacher, or program can change anyone. Only Jesus can; so each Christian must first be taught how that works.

For example, although marriage courses are great, unless those attending are first made into disciples of Jesus so that they know how to learn from Him and let Him transform them into loving Christlike spouses, they will only experience limited and/or temporary improvements in their marriage. The book of Ephesians teaches on marriage but it does so at the end of chapter five. Paul spent the first four and a half chapters laying the foundation for spiritual growth in Christ. You cannot effectively teach what Paul teaches about marriage without laying the foundations he laid in the first part of his letter.

Every important educational process must be intentional, progressive, and intensive. Becoming Christ's disciple needs that more than any other educational process because it involves more than just learning. It's a complete transformation of who you've known yourself to be through a loving relationship with Jesus. The first phase of discipleship cannot work by passive or random osmosis.

I'd like to briefly talk about one last idea that won't work: mentoring. I understand that there are many large-hearted, well-meaning people in the Body mentoring and being mentored and I don't fault the intention or the practice. If used properly it can be helpful in the second phase. However, as an approach for "making disciples," it's flawed.

Firstly, if Jesus had told the Disciples to use the one-on-one (or even the one-on-twelve) mentoring approach they would have been completely lost when 3,000 people were added to the church. Some look at what Jesus did when He was discipling the Twelve and try to emulate that, forgetting that Jesus taught that He was going to change the discipleship program from outside-in to inside-out. What you see in Jesus' ministry with His Disciples was merely a picture of what was to come; all Christians having an intimate 24/7 Master/disciple relationship with Jesus. You are NOT called to disciple (or mentor) people, you are called to make disciples for Jesus.

> But as for you, do not be called Rabbi, because you have one teacher, and you are all brothers (Matthew 23:8).

When Jesus spoke these words the Disciples were likely shocked. In the Jewish culture a disciple was to be with his master constantly and become exactly like him. When the master died his disciples were to take his place and take on disciples of their own who would call them "Rabbi/teacher" and become just like them ... and repeat. This replication had been going on in the Jewish culture for centuries. With these words that Matthew recorded, Jesus announced that discipleship would no longer work that way and let His Disciples know that they wouldn't be getting disciples of their own. Jesus was only going to be gone for three days and He didn't need anyone to replace Him as Master. The concept of mentoring is linking yourself up with someone who you think is wiser than yourself and learning from that person. Jesus ended that system. Mentoring reproduces *us;* making disciples for Jesus reproduces *Christ.*

Some believe that Paul used a mentoring-style relationship with some of the leaders he trained up such as Timothy. However, Paul never encouraged them to emulate him; he instead directed those he taught to follow Jesus like he followed Jesus (1 Corinthians 11:1; see also 1 John 2:6).

As an Apostle, part of Paul's mandate was to train and place leaders. So he spent time with them in order to teach them what he knew about following Jesus in leadership. But again, He always directed them to follow Jesus in their growth and leadership, just as he did (2 Timothy 1:13–14; 2:7–8, 15). So what appears to be mentoring was Paul teaching and training others how to follow not him, but the Master.

In the second phase of discipleship you should encourage more mature disciples to help others learn how to follow Jesus more effectively, especially in leadership training. However, following Paul's example, these relationships should be "follow Him as I am following Him" relationships.

It's really quite simple: Jesus can disciple and transform billions simultaneously, whereas, you can mentor a handful and actually transform no one. So He gave you a simple task, you are to learn to be His disciples and then show others how to do the same. In that way you can successfully make disciples even if numbers grow from 120 to 3,120 in one day. You connect new believers with Jesus and then He teaches, guides, strengthens, loves, leads, and transforms them 24/7. Then the Body grows because each part is connected to the Head and able to encourage and strengthen the other parts.

Before I understood how making disciples worked, I used to feel bad about bringing people to faith in Christ because I didn't have time to "disciple them", which to me back then meant I didn't have time to mentor them. Now I realize that we're not called to disciple or mentor anyone; we're called to make disciples for Him. So all I need is an intentional and progressive system for making disciples and a local church full of disciples who are walking with Him, growing and willing to help and encourage new believers in their growth. With that in place, I'm free to lead as many to Him as I can … 3,000 in a day would be nice!

WHAT DISCIPLES WERE TAUGHT

Several verses in the New Testament specifically show you what new converts are to be taught. In Colossians 2:6–7 Paul writes, "*Walk in Him, rooted and built up in Him and established in the faith, just as you were taught, overflowing with gratitude.*" The writer of Hebrews says that the new disciples were taught basic doctrines (repentance, faith, baptism, laying on of hands, the resurrection, and eternal judgment 6:1–2) and "*the message about righteousness*" (5:12–14).

However, in Ephesians 4, Paul gives you the best description of what he taught new converts about the mechanics of becoming a disciple of Jesus. Remember, Paul was the one who originally taught the new converts in Ephesus and raised up leaders and teachers who continued the process, so he knew what the Ephesians were taught as new converts.

> But that is not how you learned about the Messiah, assuming you heard about Him and were taught by Him, because the truth is in Jesus. You took off your former way of life, the old self that is corrupted by deceitful desires; you are being renewed in the spirit of your minds; you put on the new self, the one created according to God's likeness in righteousness and purity of the truth (Ephesians 4:20–24).

Christians need to teach and train new converts how to walk with Jesus (by grace through faith) so they can be taught by Him and transformed. You are to teach them about righteousness, purity, and the new creation; you are to teach them how to put off the old self and put on the new self, which is created in His image; you are to teach them how to have their minds renewed with God's truth. Sound familiar? The content of this book is modeled after what Paul spent much time instilling in each new convert. It's a recipe for making disciples and what you should have been taught when you were first saved.

In Matthew 28:20 Jesus commanded you to teach new disciples to live His Word. In order for anyone to live God's Word they need to be taught that Jesus made them new creations, set them free from sin, that He's at work within them teaching them and writing His Word on their hearts, and that He's promised to cause them to walk in His way and to transform them. They need to understand repentance, redemption, forgiveness, faith, grace, the power and purpose of God's Word, the renewing of the mind, and the process of putting off the old self and putting on the new creation. They must be taught this not just as concepts but as foundations for growing in their new life in Christ. And they must be given the tools they need to be transformed into His image and to walk in His plan for them. In short, new converts must be taught and trained in everything they need to know and do in order to walk with and become like Jesus.

GETTING STARTED

I was out for coffee with a well-known pastor friend, and after a lengthy conversation about discipleship in the church, he took the discussion to the next level with this question, "So how do we move churches from what we're doing now to truly making disciples?" Great question! I haven't stopped talking to God about that since then.

Most of those reading this book will not be leaders in a church. So I'd like to deal with the question from that perspective in the main text of this book. I've included some ideas and brainstorming to help church leaders start to rethink discipleship, and what that may look like in the local church, in the back of this book.

So let's look at how we can all help each other be disciples and make disciples. Please read these verses like Jesus is speaking them to you personally.

> Obey your leaders <u>and submit to them</u>... (Hebrews 13:17).
>
> Therefore I, the prisoner for the Lord, urge you to walk worthy of the calling you have received, <u>with all humility and gentleness, with patience, accepting one another in love, diligently keeping the unity of the Spirit with the peace</u> that binds us (Ephesians 4:1–3).

If you plan on talking to a leader in your church about this concept, humbly approach and ask if you can share your thoughts and don't get upset if you're not heard right away. I'm certainly not trying to talk you out of talking to your leaders, I'm just asking you to do it properly, showing them the honor they're due (1 Thessalonians 5:12–13).

That being said, remember, the Great Commission is the task of every Christian and the only way it's going to get done is if we're all working at it; we're all to do the *"work of ministry"* (Ephesians 4:12). We've severely limited the growth and effectiveness of the Church by expecting our leaders to carry us in all things spiritual. As His disciples, we are all called to share in doing His work.

The New Testament is full of instructions about what each member of the Body is to be doing to help build the Body and to increase the Kingdom. You shouldn't have to be prodded by your spiritual leaders in order to get started. The Bible assigns all of you some phase two tasks with your fellow believers (whether they attend the same church or not), that, with a little phase one improvising, can help you get started making disciples.

> Let the message about the Messiah dwell richly among you, <u>teaching and admonishing one another in all wisdom</u>, and singing psalms, hymns, and spiritual songs, with gratitude in your hearts to God (Colossians 3:16).
>
> But speaking the truth in love, let us grow in every way into Him who is the head—Christ. From Him the whole body, fitted and knit together by every supporting ligament, promotes the growth of the body for <u>building up itself in love by the proper working of each individual part</u> (Ephesians 4:15–16).

> <u>And let us be concerned about one another in order to promote love and good works</u>… encouraging each other, and all the more as you see the day drawing near (Hebrews 10:24).
>
> <u>Therefore encourage one another and build each other up</u> as you are already doing (1 Thessalonians 5:11).
>
> <u>But encourage each other daily</u>, while it is still called today, so that none of you is hardened by sin's deception (Hebrews 3:13).

Jesus said:

> "Where two or three are gathered together in My name, I am there among them" (Matthew 18:20).

Jesus wants every member of the Body to encourage each other daily, teach one another and speak, pray and sing God's Word over each other with gratitude and in worship, helping each other get filled up with His Word so their minds can be renewed. He wants you to speak the truth in love to each other and use your gifts and everything you have to help each other in your transformation. God wants you to care about the spiritual growth of others, promoting love and good works, and building each other up daily no matter where you are—in or outside of the church building. That sounds like what an amazing pastor would do but we're the ones called to do all of that for each other.

WHAT YOU CAN DO

This book contains the basic "how to be a disciple of Jesus" information that Paul taught the new converts in the churches he started. If the content of this book has caused you to better understand your faith and what it means to be His disciple, drawn you closer to God and made a difference, then you've begun your phase one experience. How many people do you know who weren't adequately made into His disciples from the start, who could be helped by this book? Make a list. Pray for them, tell them what you've been experiencing and ask them if they'd read this book if you gave them a copy. Then order the books and give them away. When they read the book they'll also begin their phase one experience and you'll have someone to grow in your transformation with.

Before this book was printed we gave digital copies to some close friends to read and review. Some of them volunteered to help finance the first print run. My church also agreed to partner with us. Together we made a list of names of those we believed could benefit from this book and we gave them a copy. You can do the same. Start by giving books to a few friends; then partner with them and work together to deliver books to a larger, combined list.

Next invite those who agree to read the book into a phase two experience with you. Start praying for them and make yourself available to talk with them as they read so that you can encourage one another. I suggest that you read this book again with them but this time spend more time with your Bible open, studying, making notes, and praying as you go; prepare yourself not only for further growth but also to teach and help others grow. As you reread you can also start writing out and compiling your topical verse-montages.

Find practical and creative ways for your group to help each other grow in transformation; you may want to get together for coffee or tea on a regular basis with those you're reading with and talk through one "Truth of Transformation" at a time or start a "Transformation Group." Agree to call, email or text each other frequently and encourage each other with verses. You could post or text the quotes at the end of each chapter under "Power Points" as regular encouragements, discussion starters, and reminders to one another. (That's why they're there.) Share your prayer montages and, like Paul exampled, start praying them for one another. You have in your hands the means to start making disciples and that's what we're called to do; and as you help others grow you'll grow even more yourself.

If you teach a home group or an adult class in your church, consider using this book. However, please remember, this is not a once-a-week-for-ten-weeks thing. Many will have just begun to get excited about the material and get started in their transformation in that time. Have your group pray about and think of ways that you can all immerse yourselves in the learning like they did in the early church. Perhaps go through the book once quickly and a second time slowly. Share your experiences and progress with one another and pray for one another. Remember, you're not finished when you've gone through the book once or twice, you're finished when you're walking with Him and being transformed; and that's when you can really start helping others.

My dream continued...

In my dream I was being shown a large apartment building with a unique covered common area in the center. At mealtime, everyone's apartments were opened up and everyone visited and ate together. It was one big happy and amazing community meal. However, I found one man almost hidden in a small room. He didn't seem to have much to share and wasn't leaving his room to receive from others. He had a Bible that he held as important but he only read the added material in the front.

I believe that the apartment building represented the Body of Christ and its different parts around the world, a diverse mix of people from different cultures, backgrounds, and denominations. What happened at meal time was everyone opening up to one another and sharing with each other what the Lord had taught them. God speaks to and through His children and His children are in every church, ministry, and denomination around the world. God doesn't decide which group of His children is "most correct" and then align Himself with them; He loves, speaks to, teaches, and reveals Himself to all of His children who receive His grace by faith.

God reveals different pieces of the big Gospel pie to people in all different parts of His Body. Why? I believe it's for several reasons: First, God doesn't read the signs above our church doors; He simply loves all who are His. Secondly, He's the only one who has all the truth. You need to stop believing that you're okay because you attend the right church, and others aren't because they don't. Finally, I believe, it's His way of moving us to unity. He hands out the different puzzle pieces to His people in Christ all over the world, and thereby rewards those who focus on unity with a greater revelation of who He is.

> I have given them the glory You have given Me. <u>May they be one as We are one</u>. I am in them and You are in Me. <u>May they be completely one, so the world may know</u> You have sent Me and have loved them as You have loved Me (John 17:22–23).

The key to making disciples of all nations is our unity. *"May they be completely one, so the world may know…"* The key to unity in the Body is everyone becoming Jesus' disciple and being transformed into His image. *"I have given them the glory You have given Me. May they be one as We are one."* When you become a disciple and begin making disciples you start reflecting and demonstrating the glory/image of God. When that happens you'll all start being one as the Father and Son are one; and when *that* happens the world will see it and know that Jesus is who He claimed to be.

We can't skip making disciples for Him, being transformed into His image and becoming one with Him and with each other, and just expect to somehow reach the nations by accident and osmosis. Make disciples, but do it with fellow believers, and strengthen and encourage each other. Do it with other churches, ministries, teachers, and denominations; pool your resources, learn from one another and help and encourage one another.

At the beginning of this book I shared a dream. In that dream I was standing on the ancient steps of a King's castle. I held a binder full of my correspondence with the King, and people were pressing in to see its contents. As I grew uncomfortable and wanted to escape, a calm onlooker, with a glance and a smile, assured me it was okay. Through that dream God showed me that He wanted me to share openly with others what He had taught me about how my transformation began. That binder is this book. I've shared it with you and now it's your turn to share what you've learned with others.

My desire and my prayer for all of you is that you would realize the amazing love and plan that the Father has for you and that you'd head towards it by walking with Jesus as His disciple, and being transformed into all God originally imagined, and what He intended when He created you. And I pray that as you go you'll be filled—in ever-increasing measure—with His Spirit, love, joy, wisdom, faith, strength, and power, and have a revolutionary impact on the people and the world around you. Rest and run and take others with you!

Here's a summary of what you've learned in this book.

It's always been God's will to create you in His image and likeness by transforming you into the image of His Son. That's the goal of your salvation. Jesus is your Master and Teacher and He's in you and with you personally, discipling and transforming you. You can be transformed because Jesus gave you His righteousness and everything else you need to be transformed as a free gift; it's all by grace. Since everything you need for life and transformation has been given to you by grace (so that it can be guaranteed) you must learn to receive it all simply by faith.

Jesus redeemed every part of you and made you completely new, so nothing can hold you back. You already are the new creation created in Christ's image and you grow up into that by putting off the old self and putting on the new self. God's Word informs and empowers your transformation. As you learn it, your mind is renewed and you're transformed. God is love and He works love in you so that you love Him, you know His love for you, and you love others as He loves them.

The centerpiece of your salvation and transformation is an amazing relationship with the Father, Son, and Holy Spirit, which you have received by grace and grow up into as you are transformed. Much of your conversation with Him centers around His loving will and purposes for you; so you pray through your transformation by relationally praying God's will with His Word which teaches you, renews your mind, strengthens you, and facilitates your transformation.

God's plan has always been to transform you into all that He envisioned and created you to be—which is beyond your imagining—in and through Christ Jesus your Savior, Teacher, and Master. You get there by believing that Jesus has already paid the price for it all, and that you already are a new creation. You also need to cooperate with the process moment by moment by faith, confident that He is at work within you, causing you to *want* to do and *do* His will, and empowering and directing your transformation.

And finally, you are to be His disciple and to help make disciples.

Help Make Disciples

Jesus has called you to be His disciples and to make disciples for Him. Here are some ways you can get started:

- Make a list and give the book away to everyone you know that would be helped by it, like we did.

- Start helping others become disciples.

- Start a "Transformation Group."

- If you have more resources than names on your list, buy books and give them to others to give away.

- Donate money to your church (or another church) for buying and giving away this book.

- Help and support your church as it steps out and starts making disciples for Him.

- If you're creative, write a transformation song, make an *At Work Within* T-shirt, etc.

- If you're on social media, start tweeting and posting the quotes at the end of each chapter under "Power Points" to encourage and help your friends. Please use #AtWorkWithin, Rick Osborne or @rickosborne after each quote. You can find more Rick Osborne quotes on Twitter @rickosborne.

- If you're a church or ministry leader interested in joining our conversation about "Making Disciples" for Him and transformation, visit our website AtWorkWithin.com.

- If you're a blogger, write a blog about this book and get people talking; if you have any questions about links or books, etc., please contact us through AtWorkWithin.com.

- If you lead a ministry and/or a media ministry and you want to talk about, promote, and/or sell this book, please contact us through AtWorkWithin.com.

- If you want to schedule Rick Osborne to speak, please contact us at AtWorkWithin.com.

- If you're an author or teacher start thinking about how the "transformation by grace through faith" message can be applied to the areas you generally teach in. Then pray about getting prepared to write, provide, and teach a topic-specific transformation course at your church.

- If you run a Bible school or provide online courses, pray about how you can practically partner with churches who want to make disciples of their whole congregation.

- If you teach children or youth, start praying and thinking about how you can teach this material to them. No one is too young to be His disciple and be transformed.

- Are you one of those wounded soldiers that God showed me a picture of? Rest and run in your transformation and ask God how you can start helping others be transformed.

- Take the 1,000-book challenge: Myself, my wife and some of our family and friends made our lists of who we thought would benefit from this book and we personally funded giving everyone on the list a copy. You might want to get together with others and do the same. If you want a copy for everyone in your church, company, ministry, community, etc., this may also work for you. You'll find the details at our store at AtWorkWithin.com.

- If you're involved in translation and foreign language publishing and you'd like to talk with someone about this book, please contact us through AtWorkWithin.com.

- If you've thought of other ways to share this book, please let us know what you did and how it worked, so others can be inspired, by contacting us through AtWorkWithin.com.

POWER POINTS
Quotes for Sharing on Social Media

Paul believed that his growth and work were empowered by God's grace and his faith was demonstrated by what he did by grace.

∼

If you remain where you are, doing what you've always done, you'll continue to get the same results.

∼

God's grace becomes effective in you when you mix in your faith and begin moving.

∼

God has given you everything you need for transformation and the core of that provision is your relationship with Him.

∼

Because of God's love for you He acts according to His grace. Because of your love for Him you act according to your faith.

∼

Your faith in His complete work should catapult you forward.

∼

The early church understood that the goal was transformation and the way to get there was to learn to walk with Jesus.

∼

The goal of the early New Testament Church was to make disciples for Jesus and they turned the world upside down.

The clear vision for the churches that Paul ministered to was that each member would become Christlike.

∽

Jesus said, "I wish that you were cold or hot." We need to be careful not to set up churches to facilitate the lukewarm.

∽

The local church is to be a boot-camp where new believers are made into Jesus' disciples and then sent out to live as He did.

∽

Jesus said He'd build His Church and He told us to make disciples. When you attempt to do His part and ignore yours, you fail.

∽

In the early church, Stephen and Philip were just regular Christians who were taught how to be Jesus' disciples.

∽

The Apostles' goal was to preach the Gospel of conversion to the unconverted and the Gospel of transformation to the converted.

∽

Paul wanted the churches to not only make disciples but to also continually raise up teachers who could do the same.

∽

Paul teaches that the ministers in the church are to be involved in "training of the saints in the work of ministry."

∽

The only way every part of His Body can help mature the Body is if all of them have first been made into disciples of Jesus.

What if our churches were full of people like the first seven deacons: true disciples of Jesus, full of His Spirit and wisdom?

~

Discipleship is not only for new believers; you never stop being His disciples and He never stops teaching and transforming you.

~

No teacher, preacher, or program can change anyone. Only Jesus can; so each Christian must first be taught how that works.

~

You are NOT called to disciple (or mentor) people, you are called to make disciples for Jesus.

~

Mentoring reproduces us; making disciples for Jesus reproduces Christ.

~

What appears to be mentoring was Paul teaching and training others how to follow not him, but the Master.

~

Jesus can disciple and transform billions simultaneously, whereas, you can mentor a handful and actually transform no one.

~

You are to learn to be His disciples and then show others how to do the same.

~

You connect new believers with Jesus and then He teaches, guides, strengthens, loves, leads, and transforms them 24/7.

New converts must be taught and trained in everything they need to know and do in order to walk with and become like Jesus.

∼

The Great Commission is the task of every Christian and the only way it's going to get done is if we're all working at it.

∼

We've severely limited the growth and effectiveness of the Church by expecting our leaders to carry us in all things spiritual.

∼

God wants you to care about the spiritual growth of others, promoting love and good works, and building each other up daily.

As you help others grow you'll grow even more yourself.

∼

God doesn't decide which group of His children is "most correct" and then align Himself with them.

∼

God reveals different pieces of the big Gospel pie to people in all different parts of His Body.

∼

God doesn't read the signs above our church doors; He simply loves all who are His.

∼

You need to stop believing that you're okay because you attend the right church, and others aren't because they don't.

The key to unity in the Body is everyone becoming Jesus' disciple and being transformed into His image.

Rest and run and take others with you!

End Notes

Brainstorming with Church Leaders

GETTING STARTED IN YOUR CHURCH

Please remember, everything I've written in this section is purely brainstorming, that will hopefully inspire your brainstorming. None of these ideas are meant to be "The New Blueprints" for church; they're not even meant to be prescriptive. My purpose is to help inspire us all to start answering the question, "How can we effectively make disciples in our churches today?" Feel free to take from these ideas, be inspired by parts of them, ignore them and/or come up with better ones. But please read, think, pray, brainstorm, and help us all move forward.

Many have studied or looked into the topic of past revivals/spiritual renewals and asked the question; "What gets them started?" I think that the more important question is, "Why do they stop?" I believe the answer is simple and practical. When revival happens, we pack our churches with new converts who have unrenewed minds and they sometimes become the majority. Unless we're focused on turning the converts into His disciples, the spiritual and social situation becomes untenable because of the flesh (*sarx*) and falls apart through strife and infighting. As we've seen, even with thousands being added to the church regularly, the early church was able to thrive because they focused on making disciples which meant the Body matured as it grew. Rapid church growth without truly making disciples is like building a skyscraper on the sand; collapse is inevitable.

Jesus never told us to pray about the harvest/revival—He makes that ready (John 4:35)—He told us to pray for more workers (Matthew 9:37–38; Luke 10:1–2). I believe Jesus told us to focus on workers because He sends "disciples" into the harvest (John 4:38) and we're the ones who are supposed to make "disciples." When you make disciples you provide workers for the Lord to send. When you don't, much of the harvest stays in the fields. Both times that Jesus told His Disciples to pray for more workers, He was sending them out into the harvest—first the Twelve then the Seventy. As Jesus sent them out He was already preparing them to think in terms of making more workers. The harvest is ready; if you want to see it come in, pray for more workers and get busy making disciples.

So how do you get started? First put aside some time in prayer specifically for this topic. Pray Paul's prayers over your church and your leadership and ask for wisdom. You may want to start sharing this book. Your next move could be to meet with key leadership (or leadership groups)—after they've read the book—and discuss ideas for changing or tweaking your church's vision. Next, you may want to do (or suggest) a series of sermons around the topic of discipleship and transformation and perhaps have a congregational meeting. (You have my permission to photocopy or reproduce parts and/or sections of this book to hand out in your church to help with discussions, meetings, and sharing the vision.)

When you're ready, the first thing you must do is to establish and communicate the vision until everyone who comes in the doors of your church clearly understands why they are there: "To be intentionally taught by my spiritual leaders how to be a disciple of Christ Jesus—knowing, loving, being taught by, and following Him; so that I can be transformed into His image, become all God created me to be and become fully equipped to impact the world and expand God's Kingdom with my life and gifts; all in partnership with my brothers and sisters in Christ."

Once you've discussed, agreed on, and started establishing the vision, the next step is to discuss designing, testing, and implementing a system that will effectively, purposely, and constantly make disciples. Obviously, it has to look different than it did in the early church because you live in a very different world. They had a different culture with different time restraints; daily five-hour classes probably won't work for your church. However, you also have some things they didn't have that can help you accommodate people's schedules: YouTube, websites, audio recordings, social media, etc. Yes, making disciples should involve personal oversight and community, but not every part of the learning needs to.

While you're praying, visioning, and brainstorming the system's details, it's important to remember what making disciples is and what it is not. Continually remind everyone involved that it's all about not only connecting each Christian to what Jesus taught, but to Him directly in a very real relationship. A vital part of *"teaching them to observe everything I have commanded you"* is teaching people what Jesus taught you about your relationship with Him: He is with you, He disciples and teaches you, you know Him and are known by Him, you hear His voice, He manifests Himself and reveals the Father to you, He works in you and with you, etc.

It's also important to remember that making disciples must involve training as well as teaching. When I was writing this book I taught the material in a class (two days a week for ten weeks). The Lord had me teach the class—from beginning to end—twice, partly because I needed to learn what was effective and what wasn't. The second time through I added several workshops that focused on practical application of the material like, "How to Hear, Know, and Walk with Jesus," "How to Learn God's Word with Jesus," "How to Put Off and Put On," "How to Pray Through Your Transformation," and more. I made the classes hands-on, interactive, and full of practical exercises. The feedback and the results were awesome.

The really cool thing is that Jesus showed up in the workshops and started to disciple each student. He told Christians to make disciples for Him so it's elementary to expect that He would work with them as they're connecting others to Him. The basic understanding of how to be His disciple is in this book and needs to be taught as a foundation, but practical how-to workshops should be added to help the students learn and experience how things work.

In order to become churches that "Make Disciples," some may be so bold as to restructure the way they do church; while some may find effective ways of refocusing by tweaking what is already normative for their congregations. I call the latter "working with the way you do church." Let's first look at some ideas that could work that way.

WORKING WITH THE WAY YOU DO CHURCH

Make becoming Jesus' disciple and transformation a personal focus for every person in your congregation while providing support and oversight. Yes, the church is supposed to make disciples, but the members are also to understand the calling and process and devote themselves to it *"And they devoted themselves to the apostles' teaching"* (Acts 2:42). Ultimately, unless a person does this, they won't become a disciple. Therefore, you can put each individual in charge of their own discipleship program (especially those who have already been Christians for some time), and provide the tools, oversight, and support they need. There are a few different ways you can do this. You can start by giving everyone in the congregation a copy of this book. In order to keep everyone on track, consider working through the book with sermons related to each section and have your home/community groups walk through the book as well.

Also, in order to activate your members in the "making disciples" process, teach a message on what I covered above about how each Christian can help others around them become disciples. Then encourage them to start doing it. That message should also be taught specifically to your home/community group leaders. Pray about and find people who can teach related practical workshops and schedule them at regular intervals in your church.

Finally, find ways to make the idea of "becoming His disciple and being transformed into His image" part of your church's DNA so it's not forgotten. Consider going through the book once a year and/or establishing an ongoing "At Work Within" or "Transformation" class. (Just don't call it a "Discipleship" class; there are too many misconceptions about that word.) This class should be for newcomers and new converts, so include this material in your newcomers/membership class. Also consider starting "Transformation Groups."

CHANGING THE WAY YOU DO CHURCH

Perhaps once you've taken the steps outlined above you may, as a church, want to consider another more radical step. Drastic change is a bold step, but some brave souls will want to discard everything that's not contributing to God's goal and start to only focus on what is. Here's just one idea that's meant to get you thinking and brainstorming—an example of something that could work:

What if going to church on Sunday morning wasn't just about doing the same thing you did last week? When you sign up for a community or college course, you're excited about attending because you know that you're going to get better at something you love and that's going to make your life better. What if church was like that? What if going to church was exciting because you were learning and progressively moving forward in your relationship with God and being ministered to at your stage of growth and at your point of need?

Picture a short worship service and a short inclusive sermon that would briefly welcome regulars and newcomers and inspire everyone. (To give you more time, announcements could be skipped by projecting them onto a screen prior to the service, sending them out via email, and putting them in the bulletin.) After the short service (50 minutes) everyone would break for coffee and fellowship (20 minutes), before splitting up into separate classes (perhaps 50 minutes). I suggest that you don't put the classes before the service; your class attendance will drop significantly and you'll lose the needed mindset of everyone involved and growing together. (If you don't have room to separate into classes you may consider still keeping your Sunday morning service short and have your classes early Sunday evening in people's homes.)

You will have already established the vision for making disciples so everyone will be on-page and ready to attend the class that is pertinent to them. Perhaps the first class would be an Alpha-type "New Believers" class; the next an "At Work Within" Transformation Class; the third class could be "Ministering To Others;" etc. Once everyone has gone through the first three or four basic classes then you could add topic-specific classes on "Marriage," "Biblical Finances," and more. (Once you understand being His disciple, the principles can be applied to every area of life.) This two-part, making-disciples focused service could easily be completed in two hours—start to finish.

If you connect your midweek home groups (Transformation Groups) to this system, those attending the same class could meet together midweek and discuss and apply Sunday's lesson. For continuity, the person who teaches the Sunday morning class could also lead the midweek one.

Sunday morning could focus on instruction and the midweek group could focus on review, discussion, training, application, and support.

I followed that twice-a-week-teaching-then-training model when I taught my "At Work Within" class and it worked really well. I also had the class members read, pray through, and study each section at home before it was taught in the class. It's hard to learn and grow in anything that's only taught once a week. For this reason, I'd highly recommend that at-home reading material be provided for each class. When the leadership in our church first discussed my "At Work Within" course, many thought that the time commitment would be too great for some (classes twice a week plus at-home reading). However, the amount of people who signed up shocked everyone and by the time the course was over no one wanted it to stop. People are hungrier than you think.

When newcomers come to your church they can be welcomed during the coffee break and invited to an appropriate newcomers' class. If they are Christians then they can be directed to a class explaining the vision of your church. Those who are not Christians can be invited to a basic Gospel class. Those who have come because of an urgent need can be taken aside to be helped through prayer and counseling. Those who just want to attend a quick service can rejoice because it was so short; they'll be back and will eventually catch the vision.

Once your members have gone through the 3–4 basic classes and are growing in their transformation, and have attended the topical classes relevant to them, they could attend a "Teachers" class and learn how to teach and/or assist in one of the classes so that teachers can be trained up and take turns teaching. And/or they could attend a "High Calling" class for those who want to encourage and help each other to press on to complete transformation. This class could run continually and could even be taught in turns by those who attend. The fruit of this class should be more ministers who can help counsel, pray for, teach, and train others in the church and disciples who are prepared to go out and bring others in.

There are different ways that children's ministry can work in this model. Firstly, the kids could attend the short worship and sermon service. A nursery and preschool area could be provided for children who can't sit through the service. While the adult Bible classes are being taught, the kids can attend children's age-appropriate Bible classes. Many churches struggle to find enough teachers for the children; this model can be designed to produce them. As you raise up more teachers, your current teachers can get a break and go through the classes. (You can even have all those who are trained as teachers cycle through and take turns teaching children.)

One last suggestion for you to think about: it seems to me like everyone, everywhere—ministries and churches—are starting casual brick-and-mortar and/or online Bible schools or classes. I'm very encouraged by this trend but I think it may be a little misdirected. I say "misdirected" because these schools and classes seem to be aimed at either the young or the highly-motivated. This audience targeting continues to do what the Church has been doing for many generations: find those who are zealous and/or "called" and ship them off to a special school so they can be taught and trained to become pastors and ministers, and then be hired to do all of the spiritual heavy-lifting for the rest of the Body.

But the truth is, we're all called to be His disciples, to learn from Him, and grow and continue the ministry of the Master. We're *all* called to be ministers. Christians in leadership are not called to make disciples and ministers of some, but of all. I believe these local and online schools are being inspired by the Lord, but I think they need to be aimed at every Christian and structured in such a way that every Believer in every church can get involved and is encouraged to do so.

Here's the idea: find courses and/or classes that are being offered online that will help your congregation in some level of their transformation. Then align your church with that school or class (applying for a group license for everyone in your church), and add the course to your Sunday morning classes and your midweek groups. As more churches partner with these online courses, more and better courses will become available. This could be a wonderful way to start for those who don't feel they have enough teachers. Or find free sermons and courses on YouTube and use them. (Christians watching sermons and courses on YouTube is a large and growing trend, so you might as well harness and direct it.) Have someone who is able lead the group, prepare discussion questions, and motivate the group to encourage one another in their growth and the application of what they're learning.

The video class will also help deal with the problem of those who work shifts or have to miss classes. The first time I taught the "At Work Within" class I set up a simple digital video camera and then downloaded the video to YouTube using a private link. Then I emailed the link to anyone who had missed the class. Once this was announced, people who would normally not sign up because of their schedules gladly came on board. Videoing your classes can also help you repeat the courses without stretching your available teachers; you just need a teacher-in-training who can guide the class.

I believe that if you're effectively making disciples for Him, your churches will look more like ministry training centers than what they look like now. Churches should be boot-camps just buzzing with the talk and reality of everyone being connected with Jesus, being trained how to follow Him, being transformed from glory to glory into His image, and then going out to impact their areas of influence for the Kingdom.

Again, these are all just ideas that have been brainstormed in order to give you a launching pad for your own brainstorming. What works for one church may not work for the next. Get your leaders together, pray, brainstorm, and decide to move forward. Then schedule it, test it, and tweak it as you go. Don't wait until you have the perfect model before you start. And don't wait until you have all of the classes in a nice little organized progression before you start. No matter how good what you develop is, it'll get better as you roll it out, test it, make changes, and add to it. So let it grow as your church does. Just don't ever lose sight of the purpose, to "Make Disciples" for Him.

Let's all work on this together and help each other get back to making disciples for Jesus. I welcome your ideas. Once you're up and going please visit our website AtWorkWithin.com and e-mail me what you're trying and how it's working.

POWER POINTS
Quotes for Sharing on Social Media

Rapid church growth without truly making disciples is like building a skyscraper on the sand; collapse is inevitable.

∽

When you make disciples you provide workers for the Lord to send. When you don't, much of the harvest stays in the fields.

∽

The harvest is ready; if you want to see it come in, pray for more workers and get busy making disciples.

∽

We're all called to be His disciples, to learn from Him, and grow and continue the ministry of the Master.

∽

Christians in leadership are not called to make disciples and ministers of some, but of all.

∽

Churches should be boot-camps just buzzing with the talk and reality of everyone being connected with Jesus.